YOUR BODY

An A-Z from ALLERGIES to ZITS

Steve Parker

A & C Black • London

First published in 2005 by
A&C Black Publishers Ltd
38 Soho Square
London W1D 3HB

www.acblack.com

Text copyright © Steve Parker

Consultant: Dr Rashmin Tamnhe,
Consultant Paediatrician, Leicester City West PCT
Honorary Senior Lecturer in Child Development
and Behaviour, University of Leicester

Cover illustrations and cartoons by Jon Davis
Other illustrations by Peter Bull
Design by Sharyn Troughton
Edited by Veronica Ross and Mary-Jane Wilkins

ISBN 0-7136-7192-0

A CIP catalogue for this book is available
from the British Library

A&C Black uses paper produced with elemental
chlorine-free pulp, harvested from managed
sustained forests

Printed in Great Britain by Creative Print
and Design (Wales), Ebbw Vale

INTRODUCTION

We all have a body to live in, use every day and look after. In this A-Z of the human body you will find:

- **Descriptions of body parts, from microscopic cells to major organs such as the liver and lungs.**
- **Explanations of how important body parts work, and how they are involved in processes such as breathing and digesting food.**
- **Information about how our bodies go wrong when we have illnesses and diseases. In particular we include illnesses which especially affect younger people and those we can prevent by our own actions.**
- **Topics relating to health care and the people who carry it out, such as doctors, nurses and physiotherapists.**

How to use this book

You can use this A-Z in several ways. You might simply flick through its pages and read whatever catches your eye. Some topics can be explained in just a few lines. More important ones about vital body bits, such as the brain and heart, naturally take up more space.

Perhaps you've heard of a body part or an illness, and you want to know more. You can look it up in its alphabetical position. If it's not there, use the index at the end.

Some detailed terms are grouped under a more general heading. For example, retina is explained under eye.

Most topics have a *See also* list. You can scan through this first, to check whether the information might be on another page. Or you could follow up a particular aspect of a subject using one of the *See also* headings. Further sources of information are listed on page 158.

Into action

Learning about our own bodies, the way they work, and what might go wrong, is fascinating and worthwhile. It gives us knowledge and understanding. But we need to act on our knowledge and perhaps change what we do and say, as well as the choices we make every day.

Doctors and modern health care can do amazing things. But we cannot hand over responsibility for our bodies and assume that medicine fixes everything. This book tries to add to your knowledge and to help you keep your body healthy, happy and working well.

ABDOMEN

See also Bladder, Intestines, Kidneys, Liver, Sexual Organs, Sexual Reproduction, Stomach

The abdomen is the lower half of the main body or torso. The upper half of the body is the chest. The abdomen contains mainly the intestines or guts, liver and pancreas, and the kidneys and bladder which get rid of wastes. In the female body it also contains the reproductive or sexual parts. The abdomen is sometimes called the tummy or belly.

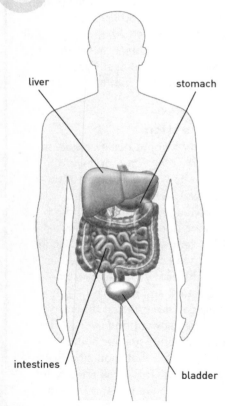

liver
stomach
intestines
bladder

The abdomen is between the chest and the hips.

ABORTION

See also Birth, Embryo, Pregnancy

Abortion happens when an embryo or foetus – a baby at an early stage of development – leaves the womb and does not survive. It may happen naturally, due to a problem in development of the embryo or foetus. This is called spontaneous abortion or miscarriage. It can also happen in an operation, perhaps to save the life of the mother if she is suddenly very ill in pregnancy. This is known as planned abortion or termination. It should always be carried out by doctors or similar experts.

There are medical guidelines which allow terminations only during a certain stage of pregnancy. The decision to have a termination can be very difficult, and requires much thought and discussion with expert advisers.

ABSCESS

See also Antibiotics, Germs

An abscess is a collection, pool or lump of fluid called pus, which is the result of infection with germs. An abscess can be anywhere in the body. It may cause swelling, tenderness and even great pain, for example, a tooth abscess. If an abscess bursts, it may spread pus and infection to nearby areas. Abscesses can be treated by a small operation to remove the pus, and perhaps antibiotic drugs to fight the infection.

ACCIDENTS AND EMERGENCIES

See also Bites and Stings, Bleeding, Burns, Choking, Fainting, First Aid, Heart, Hypothermia

Some emergencies are obvious, for example a serious car accident. Others are not, for example the person who looks pale and feels faint because he is having a heart attack. In an emergency situation it's important to get proper help as quickly as you can – you could save a life.

First aid

First-aiders are trained to assess a situation fast, to act at once if someone's life is in immediate danger, and to get expert help as quickly as possible. For people who are not trained in first aid, the best action is to find someone who is. This could mean phoning 999 for emergency services.

Faints and falls

A person who feels faint should lie down before they fall down and injure themselves. You should not move an injured person (especially after a fall) unless life is in danger, for example if there is a fire or poisonous gas nearby. First-aiders are trained to save lives, but also not to take risks that might mean they become casualties themselves.

Comfort and recovery

A first-aider stays with a casualty until paramedics or other professionals arrive. They may need to put a casualty into the recovery position, lying partly on one side with one arm and leg straight, and the other arm and leg bent. This helps to prevent further injury and stops an injured person choking on vomit.

The recovery position helps to keep an injured person safe and stable until help arrives.

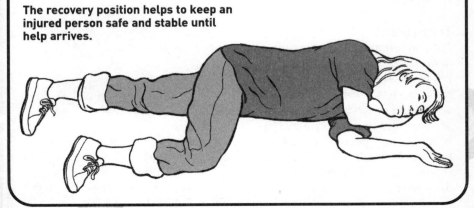

ACNE

See also Boils, Hormones, Puberty,
Skin and Touch, Spots and Skin Marks

Acne is the term for spots and pimples on the skin. It usually happens because of hormone changes during puberty and the teenage years. Acne can affect the face, neck, back, chest and upper arms. There's no medical evidence that certain foods cause it. However, an unhealthy diet and lifestyle (for example eating too many fatty foods and staying up late every night) may worsen the skin's overall condition.

Acne spots

Each spot is a tiny pore or follicle from which a hair grows. The pore or follicle also contains a sebaceous gland, which makes natural oils and waxes called sebum to keep skin supple. Hormones can make the glands produce too much oil and wax. This collects as a small swelling or bulge, forming a spot or pimple. Occasionally the spot becomes infected with pus, and is called a boil.

Treatment

Picking or squeezing spots makes acne worse and may cause an infection. The main treatment is to wash well twice daily with anti-acne soap or lotion. People with acne should try not to worry too much – many people suffer from it and good friends will sympathize. Doctors can prescribe a medical drug for serious cases.

ADENOIDS

See also Nose and Smell,
Lungs and Breathing

The adenoids are two slightly bulging areas at the back of the inside of the nose. They fight germs and may swell during an infection. Some people's adenoids swell often, which makes breathing through the nose difficult. The swelling also affects speech and increases the risk of coughs and ear infections too. Having adenoids really means having swollen adenoids. If they are a long-term problem, they can be treated by an antibiotic drug or removed in an operation.

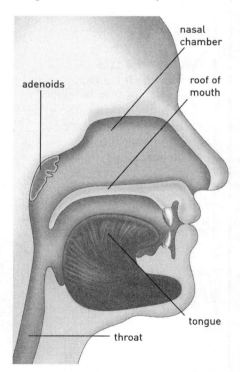

Adenoids are at the lower rear of the nasal chamber.

ADHD

See also Brain and Thinking, Doctors,
Learning Difficulties

ADHD is Attention-Deficit/
Hyperactivity Disorder. It's a
medical condition affecting the
workings of the brain's natural
chemicals. This in turn affects
behaviour. ADHD sometimes
runs in families.

Attention deficit

Someone with attention deficit
tends to be easily distracted,
has limited concentration, is
forgetful and loses things.
Hyperactivity involves fidgeting,
interrupting, getting agitated,
and being endlessly 'on the go',
unable to relax for long.
   Some people behave like this
now and then, but if they have
ADHD their behaviour is more
extreme and long-lasting. It can
affect learning, making friends
and social life.

Treatment

Treating ADHD is usually a team
effort involving parents and family,
and various doctors such as
paediatricians (child specialists),
neurologists (nerve and brain
specialists), psychiatrists and
psychologists (experts on the
mind), as well as teachers and
behaviour therapists. There are
various medical drugs to help
the condition. With the right team,
treatment and support, ADHD
can be controlled. About half the
children who show the effects of
ADHD grow out of it by adulthood.

ADRENALS AND ADRENALINE

See also Glands, Hormones, Kidneys

The adrenals are two hormone-
making glands, one on top of
each kidney. The outer layer
or cortex makes corticosteroid
hormones that control the body's
water balance, energy use and
response to stress. The inner part
or medulla makes adrenaline.
This gets the body ready for
action by speeding heartbeat
and breathing, making more
blood flow to the muscles and
less blood go to the skin and guts.

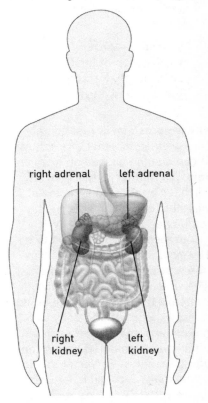

right adrenal   left adrenal

right kidney   left kidney

**Each adrenal gland is pyramid-
shaped and lies above the kidney.**

7

AIDS AND HIV

See also Blood, Germs and Infection,
Immunity and Immunizations, Injections,
Sex, Tattoos, Viruses

HIV stands for Human Immunodeficiency Virus. It is the virus that causes AIDS, Acquired Immune Deficiency Syndrome.

- **Acquired – AIDS is caused by acquiring the virus HIV.**

- **Immune – HIV affects the body's self-defence immune system.**

- **Deficiency – the immune system does not work properly.**

- **Syndrome – AIDS is a group or collection of health problems that occur together. This is called a syndrome.**

HIV is spread by sexual contact (not ordinary contact or kissing). It can also be passed on from an infected mother to her baby at birth, or by sharing syringes or needles (used to inject drugs) with a person who has HIV.

A person with HIV is said to be HIV-positive, even though he or she may seem healthy at first. The virus affects the immune system's lymphocyte white blood cells. As a result, the body can no longer protect itself against infections such as TB, pneumonia and meningitis. Powerful medical drugs make it possible for people to live with HIV for years, but a cure has not yet been found.

ALCOHOL

See also Drugs, Health Risks

People have drunk alcohol for thousands of years, and many can enjoy an occasional alcoholic drink without any problems. But alcohol is a depressant drug that slows down the workings of the brain. A little alcohol can make people feel happy, relaxed and friendly. But too much causes many problems including slurred speech, confusion, loss of balance, vomiting, mood swings and violence.

Someone who drinks a lot of alcohol over a long period may become dependent or addicted to the drug. This can lead to diseases of the liver, heart and pancreas, as well as social difficulties such as debt and relationship breakdown. Doctors and groups such as Alcoholics Anonymous (AA) or Alateen provide advice and treatment for people with alcohol problems.

WHAT PEOPLE SAY

I feel much more alert after a few drinks.
Maybe people feel this inside. But even one drink can slow reactions, affect concentration and increase the risk of an accident.

Saying no

It can be tempting to try alcohol, to see what it's like and because others are doing it. But drinking alcohol is dangerous, and illegal in many places if you are under 18. If friends try to pressure you into having a drink, say no and seek advice from a teacher or an adult you trust. Alcohol can make you feel sick and make you do embarrassing things. It may get you into trouble with parents, school, work or the police. Too much can lead to alcohol poisoning, which can kill.

ALLERGIES

See also Asthma, Eczema, Food Poisoning, Hay Fever, Immunity and Immunizations, Rashes, Spots and Skin Marks

The body's immune system normally fights germs and disease. But occasionally the immune system attacks harmless substances, such as grass pollen, or some foods which have no effect on most people, to provoke an allergic reaction. Almost any substance can trigger an allergy, from metals such as nickel to plants or foods such as peanuts. A tendency to allergies seems to run in families, but there is no way to predict this. Some people are allergy-prone, with several allergic conditions.

Allergens

The substance that causes an allergy is an allergen (antigen). The body becomes extra-sensitive or sensitized (hypersensitive) to the allergen and the immune defence system reacts against it. Certain kinds of microscopic cells, known as mast cells, release substances called histamines and prostaglandins. These cause swelling, redness, itching and other symptoms in various body parts – not always the ones in contact with the allergen. For example, a food allergy may show itself as swellings on the skin.

What to do

Once an allergen is identified, the best treatment is prevention – stay away from the source of the reaction as much as possible. There are medical drugs, such as antihistamines, that reduce the original allergic reaction. There are also treatments such as eyewashes to soothe itchy eyes brought on by hay fever, and airway-widening aerosol sprays for asthma. A doctor can advise on these, and recommend a specialist allergy clinic for more detailed advice and treatment.

Severe allergic reaction

A severe allergic reaction can be life-threatening. Symptoms include swelling and redness on the skin, especially around the face, and difficulty in breathing. In rare cases the person may collapse. This condition, anaphylaxis or anaphylactic shock, is an emergency and needs urgent medical help.

ANAEMIA
*See also Blood, Oxygen,
Periods and Menstrual Cycle*

Anaemia is the name for a range
of disorders which affect the
blood's ability to carry oxygen.
Causes include poor nutrition, or
losing blood, for example from
heavy periods or a stomach ulcer.
Some types are caused by a
problem with haemoglobin, the
substance in red blood cells that
carries oxygen around the body.
Haemoglobin contains iron, and
the body needs regular supplies of
iron from food to make new red
cells. Lack of iron causes iron-
deficiency anaemia.

Pernicious anaemia occurs
when the body cannot take in
enough vitamin B12. This is also
needed to make new red cells.
Haemolytic anaemia happens
when red cells are broken down
too quickly. Sickle-cell anaemia
is inherited. The sickle-shaped
red cells are misshapen and
block tiny blood vessels.

General signs of anaemia are
paleness, tiredness, weakness,
feeling faint and short of breath.
Treatment depends on the type
of anaemia, for example, more
iron-rich foods or iron supplement
pills for iron-deficiency anaemia.

ANAESTHETICS
See also Hospitals, Operations

Anaesthesia is lack of feeling or
sensation – especially pain. Local
anaesthetics, usually given by
injection, numb part of the body.

They are used by dentists and by
doctors when stitching wounds.
An epidural is a local anaesthetic
which goes into the lower spine
(back) through an injection, for
pain relief during birth or
operations on the lower body.
When someone is given a general
anaesthetic for a major operation
they are made unconscious for
the duration of the operation.
The anaesthetic is given through
an injection, passed into the
bloodstream as a drip, or
breathed in as a gas.

ANKLE
*See also Bones and Skeleton, Joints,
Sprains*

The ankle joint has seven small
bones that slide and twist against
each other. A sprained ankle hurts
and swells rapidly. If someone has
very little movement in their
ankle, the bones look misshapen,
and they are in great pain, they
should seek urgent medical advice
in case the ankle is broken.

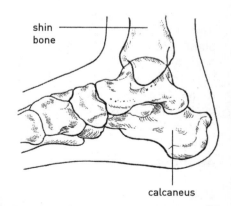

shin
bone

calcaneus

**The rearmost lower ankle bone
is the calcaneus or heel bone.**

ANOREXIA AND BULIMIA
See also Diets and Dieting, Food and Digestion, Growing, Weight

Anorexia is loss of appetite. A person with anorexia nervosa eats too little and becomes very thin, losing a quarter or more of normal body weight. Anorexia is most common in young girls; some are affected slightly, other much more. It may have several complicated causes, such as a fear of gaining weight, a desire to look like slim, famous people, worries about growing up or a desire to gain attention.

However, people with anorexia may not recognize these feelings and often believe that nothing is wrong with them. They may find clever ways of disguising the problem, such as hiding food or wearing baggy clothes.

Effects
Anorexia nervosa can cause serious problems, such as anaemia, poor skin and swollen ankles and can stop periods (amenorrhoea). It may also cause heart and blood pressure problems, and even sudden death from irregular heartbeats. Several other medical conditions can cause similar problems, so a doctor checks for them first.

Bulimia
People with bulimia nervosa eat huge amounts of food during binging sessions, then get rid of it by deliberately vomiting or taking laxatives. This can cause burns in the gullet and rotten teeth which are affected by the stomach acid in vomit.

Treatment
People with these conditions need care, love and support from their family and friends. They usually need treatment over a long time, perhaps years, by a medical team, which includes a psychiatrist.

ANTIBIOTICS
See also Bacteria, Drugs, Germs and Infection

Antibiotic drugs attack bacterial germs, but not illnesses caused by viruses such as colds and measles. Many antibiotics have names ending in -cillin, such as penicillin and amoxycillin. Doctors try not to prescribe antibiotics too often, as this may allow new kinds of bacteria to develop which are resistant to them. A course of antibiotics should be completed. Taking only some of the pills can cause further problems.

ANTIBODIES
See also Allergies, Germs and Infection, Immunity and Immunizations

Antibodies are substances made by the body's immune system to protect against germs and disease. The antibodies stick to germs and kill or disable them. Antibodies are also produced in allergies and similar body reactions.

ANTISEPTICS
See also Bacteria, Germs and Infection, Personal Hygiene, Viruses

An antiseptic is a substance that kills or damages microbes, but leaves the body unharmed. Microbes include germs such as viruses, bacteria and protists (protozoa). Antiseptics should be used for cleaning skin cuts and wounds, especially if they contain dust or dirt. They are also used by medical staff, for example, before an injection, or before incising (cutting) the skin for an operation.

APPENDIX
See also Diarrhoea, Fever, Intestines, Stomach and Digestion, Vomiting

The appendix (vermiform appendix) is a hollow pocket at the start of the large intestine, in the front lower right of the abdomen. Its exact role is not clear and for most people it causes no trouble. Occasionally it may swell, for example, if partly-digested food becomes stuck or if it becomes infected by germs. This swelling is appendicitis and as it worsens it causes great tenderness (usually at the site of the appendix but sometimes nearby), loss of appetite, fever, nausea and vomiting, and diarrhoea or constipation.

Removal
In some cases the problem may come and go in a mild form as a grumbling appendix, which can be difficult to identify. But appendicitis can quickly become a medical emergency. If a swollen appendix bursts, it may spread germs and inflammation to the general abdominal lining. This is called peritonitis. If this condition occurs, the appendix is removed in an urgent appendectomy operation.

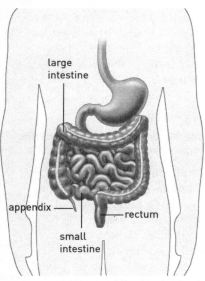

large intestine

appendix

rectum

small intestine

The appendix is a finger-shaped part of the large intestine.

WHAT PEOPLE SAY

It didn't hurt when the doctor pressed over my appendix, but when she let go.

This is often true with appendicitis. It is called rebound tenderness and is a sign that doctors look for to identify the condition.

ARTERIES
See also Bleeding, Blood Vessels, First Aid

Arteries are strong, thick-walled tubes or vessels that carry blood away from the heart. Blood travels through arteries under great pressure so it spurts out fast from a cut or wound.

If someone cuts an artery, cover the wound with something clean and press firmly on it. This should help to slow the blood flow, while you waiting for emergency help to arrive.

WHAT PEOPLE SAY

The cut couldn't be bleeding from an artery – the blood wasn't bright red.

Arterial blood is not always bright red. The pulmonary arteries from the heart to the lungs carry dark, low-oxygen blood on its way to pick up fresh oxygen.

ARTHRITIS
See also Bones and Skeleton, Joints, Rheumatism

The word arthritis is a general term for stiffness, aches and pains in the joints. It usually means the medical condition of osteoarthritis, which is described under the general term rheumatism.

ASPIRIN
See also Drugs, Fever, Paracetamol

Aspirin is:

- **anti-inflammatory, reducing redness and swelling;**
- **antipyretic, reducing fever (high body temperature);**
- **analgesic, reducing certain kinds of pain.**
- **Aspirin also helps prevent problems such as strokes and heart attacks.**

Aspirin is known chemically as acetyl-salicylic acid, and is in many over-the-counter pills, and other preparations. People with digestive ulcers should not take aspirin, as it can worsen stomach bleeding. Paracetamol is usually given to children under 12, rather than aspirin.

ASTHMA
See page 14

AUTISM
See also Brain and Thinking

A person with autism has difficulty in talking to others, making friends or forming relationships in the normal way. He or she may seem withdrawn, and may have speech problems. People with autism sometimes feel the need to do something many times, which is a form of obsessive-compulsive disorder. Treatment is complicated and long-term, and involves care, support and behaviour therapy.

ASTHMA

See also Allergies, Lungs and Breathing

Asthma is a condition that affects the body's airways. A person who has an asthma attack finds breathing difficult and is wheezy. This happens for a time and then the person is well again.

Asthma is mainly an allergic reaction to a breathed-in substance or allergen such as dust of various kinds, tiny bits of fur, hair or feathers from animals and birds, plant pollen and particles, fumes from chemicals, plastics and paints, and many other sources.

In house dust, the cause is often the droppings of the almost-invisible house dust mite. These dry out, turn to powder and float in the air. Suddenly breathing in cold air, activity such as sport, or an infection can also set off, or trigger, an asthma attack.

Treatment

In Britain, asthma affects between one in four and one in ten people, depending on where you live. Some people have an occasional mild episode. Others suffer whenever their allergen is around – yet may grow out of the condition by their teens or twenties.

Like most allergies, the keys are to avoid the allergens and treat the problem quickly. There are two main kinds of asthma inhalers (also called aerosols, sprays or puffers). One kind is

preventative or prophylactic, and is used regularly even if there is no breathlessness. The other kind widens or dilates the lungs' small airways (bronchioles) during an attack, and is known as a bronchodilator.

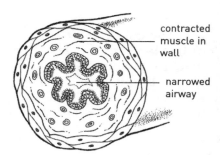

contracted muscle in wall

narrowed airway

In asthma, bronchioles become narrowed or constricted inside.

WHAT PEOPLE SAY

I only seem to get asthma when I've forgotten my inhaler.

This can be true for some people. Being worried or anxious, for example because you have forgotten your inhaler may make an asthma attack more likely.

BABIES
See pages 16–17

BACK
See also Bones and Skeleton,
Cartilage, Exercise, Joints, Neck

The backbone or spine (spinal
column) is a row of 26 bones
called vertebrae, linked by
complicated joints. A cushion-like
pad of cartilage (the intervertebral
disc) sits between each pair of
vertebrae. Movement is small
at each joint but adds up along
the whole backbone so some
people can bend double.

Back problems
People are likely to suffer
backaches and strains if they do
not exercise, if they are overweight,
or if they lift heavy objects wrongly.
This can result in a prolapsed or
slipped disc. The disc is squashed
outwards and presses on a nearby
nerve. This causes pain which
may seem to come from further
along the nerve, for example in
an arm or a leg.

How to lift safely
• **Test the weight – if it's heavy,**
get help.
• **Keep your back as straight**
as possible.
• **Bend your knees to lower your**
body; straighten them to lift.
• **Face the front and do not**
twist while lifting.
• **Put the item down in the**
same way.

Doctors and physiotherapists can
advise on treatment. Some back
sufferers gain great relief from
physical massage or manipulation
by an osteopath or chiropractor.

BACTERIA
See also Antibiotics, Germs and Infection,
Personal Hygiene, and various bacterial
infections ranging from Boils to Pneumonia,
Meningitis and Tuberculosis

DID YOU KNOW?

Each of us has friendly,
helpful bacteria called E. coli
in our intestines — enough to
fill two or three teacups.
However, some rarer types or
strains of E.coli can turn nasty
and cause problems such as
food poisoning.

Bacteria are microscopic living
things – 50,000 would fit into this
o. They are many different shapes
such as balls (cocci), rods (bacilli)
and corkscrews (spirochaetes).
Harmful bacteria are called germs
or bugs. They enter the body in
breathed-in air, through cuts in
the skin, or in food and drink.
Once inside they may multiply,
doubling in number every half-
hour or less, and causing disease.
The main weapons against
bacteria are prevention by
personal hygiene, the body's
natural immune defence system
and antibiotic drugs.

BABIES AND INFANTS

See also Antibodies, Birth, Choking, Fever, Growing, Immunity and Immunizations, Pregnancy

Babies are many things – endearing, cuddly, rewarding, joyous, but also a massive responsibility, often very tiring and sometimes a great worry. An infant is a baby under one year old. In this first year, most babies almost triple their birth weight, from an average of 3.4 to 9.9 kilograms, and grow in height from 55 to 75 centimetres. But no baby is average. Each grows and develops new actions, such as smiling, crawling and walking, at its own pace and in its own way.

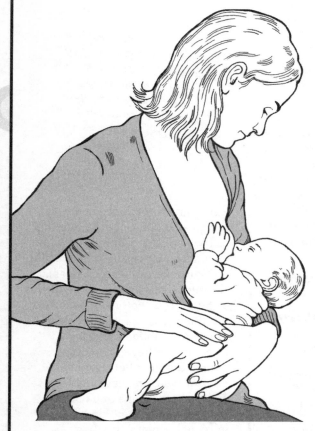

Breastfeeding is a relaxing time when mother and baby strengthen their relationship.

New mothers are encouraged to have regular post-natal (after birth) checks for themselves and their babies. A midwife, health visitor, childcare nurse or family doctor can keep an eye on the baby's progress and advise on worries. Breastfed new babies have some protection against disease in the form of substances called antibodies in their mother's milk.

As a baby grows, it can be given immunizations which protect it against serious diseases such as measles and polio. Any doubts about a baby's health or progress should be discussed with a health visitor, doctor or childcare health worker. More than nine times out of ten, all that's needed is reassurance.

Problems

Doctors who specialize in the problems of babies and children are called paediatricians. A baby's body does not deal with certain kinds of illness in the same way as an adult, and so babies need close monitoring and sometimes special care. For example, a baby may develop a fever much faster than an adult, and is more likely to have fits caused by high temperature, known as febrile fits. Also a baby who is often sick (vomits) risks losing fluids (dehydration), vital body salts and minerals within several hours.

Almost all babies naturally stuff things in their mouths, as a way of developing their coordination and exploring tastes and textures. So small items such as peanuts and marbles which may cause choking are a danger. Ill babies and young children should see a doctor or nurse sooner rather than later.

The developing baby

Medical staff used to record infant milestones of development. But each baby grows and develops at its own speed. For example, some babies miss out stages such as crawling and may shuffle on their bottoms instead, or go straight from sitting to walking.

Today, parents are encouraged to share information with medical workers about how their baby is changing day by day, week by week and month by month.

Babies' actions and skills

The ages given here are general guides only.

- **Smiles in response to faces and noises: 4-8 weeks**

- **Raises head and shoulders when lying face-down: 2-4 months**

- **Rolls over from face-down on to back: 5-7 months**

- **Starts to make babbling baby noises: 6-8 months**

- **Sits unsupported: 6-8 months**

- **Crawls at speed: 8-10 months**

- **Stands when holding on to something, such as furniture: 10-12 months**

- **Says simple words such as dada, cat, moon: 11-13 months**

- **Stands unsupported: 11-13 months**

- **Walks without help: 14-16 months**

- **Understands simple sentences, such as 'eat your food': 16-18 months**

BAD BREATH
See also Body Odour, Personal Hygiene, Teeth

When we eat, bits of food get stuck on and between our teeth. Bacteria in the mouth feed on and rot the bits, and coat the tongue and mouth lining.
All this gives breathed-out air a smell or odour – bad breath or halitosis. A person with bad breath becomes used to the smell and may not notice it. That person may well be grateful if a friend tactfully mentions it. The problem can be lessened by better oral hygiene – brushing teeth properly at least twice a day, flossing between the teeth, and rinsing with anti-bacterial mouthwashes.

BALANCE
See also Ears and Hearing, Senses

Our ability to balance lets us move about or keep still without falling over. Balance is sometimes called the body's sixth sense. In fact, it is a process involving several senses.

Hearing and balance
Deep inside each ear are three fluid-filled, semicircular canals. At the base of each canal is a clump of tiny hairs. As the head moves, the fluid swishes around. The tiny hairs sense how much the liquid moves and send messages to the brain. Your brain can then tell you which way you are moving.

Balance and sight
The eyes see horizontal and vertical lines and objects. These provide your brain with visual clues that help you balance. For example,the surface of a pond or lake is exactly level and buildings are aligned up and down.

Touch and balance
Touch sensors in the skin help too. For example, the soles of the feet can feel if the body is leaning.

All this sensory information goes continuously to the brain, which moves the muscles to control the body's position.

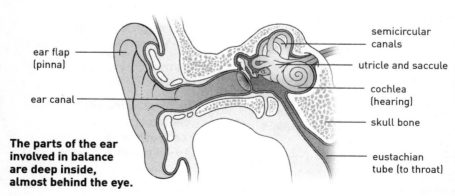

ear flap (pinna)

ear canal

semicircular canals

utricle and saccule

cochlea (hearing)

skull bone

eustachian tube (to throat)

The parts of the ear involved in balance are deep inside, almost behind the eye.

BCG
See also Tuberculosis

BCG (Bacillus Calmette-Guérin) is the name of the vaccine which is injected to make the body better able to resist the infection TB or tuberculosis, which can cause serious lung disease.

BIRTH
See pages 20–21

BIRTHMARKS
See also Skin, Spots and Skin Marks

Some babies are born with different-coloured spots or patches on their skin, known as birthmarks. They can be anywhere and any size. Usually a birthmark is harmless and it may fade over the years. Some birthmarks can be covered with cosmetic cream. Others can be removed in a small operation. A birthmark that suddenly changes in size or colour should be shown to a doctor.

BITES AND STINGS
See also Accidents and Emergencies

A sting or bite hurts for a time, but usually fades in an hour or two, although bee and wasp stings can be painful. Anti-histamine cream helps them to go. But if the bitten part swells up fast, and the person feels faint, this could be a serious reaction called anaphylaxis, which needs emergency medical help. A sting in the mouth may affect breathing and should be treated as an emergency.

BLADDER
See also Bile, Kidneys, Urine

Bladders are bag-like containers for liquids. The gall bladder under the liver stores bile. What we call the bladder is the urinary bladder in the lower body, which is shaped like a wrinkled pear. It slowly fills with urine, until tiny stretch sensors in its wall tell you that it needs emptying, which involves urinating (peeing or weeing). This usually happens when the bladder holds 200–300 millilitres of urine.

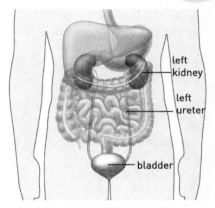

left kidney

left ureter

bladder

The bladder is the lowest part inside the main body.

WHAT PEOPLE SAY

If I can't go soon, I'll burst!
Emptying the bladder, called urination or weeing, happens long before it could tear or burst. But holding on to urine for too long could strain it for a time.

BIRTH

See also Babies and Infants, Pregnancy, Womb

A baby leaves its mother's womb at birth. Birth may take less than an hour or more than a day, and the mother may feel short discomfort or be in pain for many hours. Birth is usually quicker and easier if the mother has had babies before. Some mothers want to give birth at home, helped by a midwife. Others prefer to be in hospital, with doctors and medical equipment nearby. Birth can be very stressful and emotional, but usually has a joyous ending.

When the mother goes into labour, she feels the contractions of her womb muscles as they try to push out the baby. The womb opening or cervix begins to widen or dilate. The contractions grow stronger and more frequent. The thin bag around the baby breaks, and fluid leaks out of the womb. This is the waters breaking.

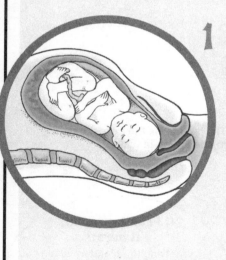

1 The cervix widens or dilates, and the baby's head engages. Contractions of the womb become stronger and more frequent.

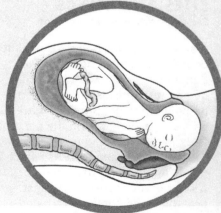

2 The baby's head passes through the cervix and vagina (birth canal) and is visible, which is called crowning.

Delivery

The mother may breathe a special gas or have medical drugs to ease the pain. The cervix widens more, and contractions push the baby out along the birth canal. After a few more contractions (or pushing), the baby is born. It usually cries, which helps to open its airways so it can breathe. More contractions push out the afterbirth (placenta).

Problems

Most babies are born head first. Sometimes the baby is in another position, such as breech (bottom-first). The doctor may try to press from the outside and turn the baby, or use spoon-like forceps to ease it out.

A Caesarean birth means that the baby is delivered through an opening cut in the mother's skin and womb wall.

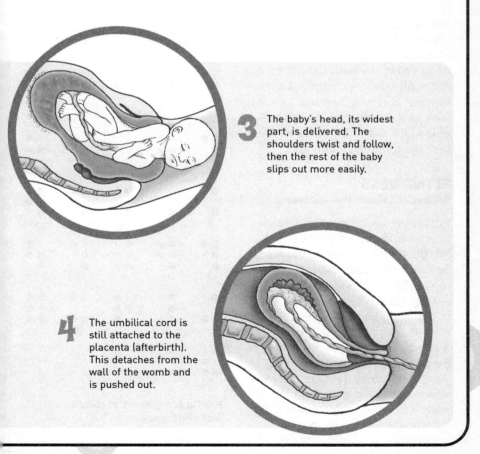

3 The baby's head, its widest part, is delivered. The shoulders twist and follow, then the rest of the baby slips out more easily.

4 The umbilical cord is still attached to the placenta (afterbirth). This detaches from the wall of the womb and is pushed out.

BLEEDING

See also Accidents and Emergencies, Blood, Blood Vessels, Bruises, First Aid

Bleeding happens when blood leaks out of its tubes or blood vessels. A few drops of blood oozing from a small cut can be covered with a sticking plaster or a dressing and bandage. The blood naturally goes sticky, or clots, and seals the leak. When bleeding is severe (haemorrhage) blood gushes out too fast to clot. A first-aider should press a dressing or pad on the wound to slow the leak until emergency help arrives.

Internal bleeding under the skin causes a bruise, but bleeding deep inside the body cannot be seen. After an injury that causes internal bleeding, someone might look pale and feel faint, with a fast pulse and shallow breathing. Then they need medical help fast.

BLINDNESS

See also Disabilities, Eyes and Seeing

People who have impaired vision or are blind see poorly or not at all. Blindness has various causes. Sometimes a baby is born unable to see. Some diseases affect eyesight, such as glaucoma. In this condition the fluid inside the eye presses on its interior. It can be treated with eye drops, medical drugs or an operation.

Accidents may damage the eyes, which is why it's important to wear a mask, goggles or visor if there's a risk to vision.

As people grow older their eyesight may naturally become misty or blurred. A cataract is a misting or fogging of the eye's lens. This can usually be treated by an operation.

People who cannot see often carry a white stick, partly to feel the way, and partly so that other people can see their condition. Some have a guide dog to help them get around. Some blind people may appreciate an offer of help – the blind person is usually guided by touching the helper's arm as the helper leads the way. Most blind people are just as clever or intelligent as other people, and appreciate being treated as such.

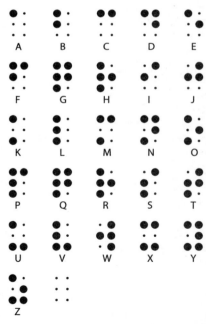

Braille is a system of raised dots that blind people can feel to read.

BLOOD

See also Anaemia, Arteries, Bleeding, BloodGroups, Blood Vessels, Bones and Skeleton, Cells, Dialysis, Donors, Haemophilia, Heart and Pulse, Hormones, Oxygen, Veins

Blood is the red liquid which is pumped by the heart round the body. It flows in tubes called blood vessels. Blood carries important substances such as oxygen and nutrients to all body parts. It collects waste substances for removal, it clots to seal wounds, and it has many other jobs.

Just over half of blood is a pale yellow watery liquid called plasma. This carries most of the nutrients and wastes. The rest is tiny cells of three main kinds. Red cells are shaped like doughnuts. They carry oxygen and give blood its colour. White cells can change their shape as they fight germs and diseases. Platelets help blood to go sticky and clot. Inside this letter o you could fit 20 million red cells, 20,000 white cells and one million platelets.

Blood pressure

Every time the heart beats, blood is squeezed into the blood vessels and presses on their walls as it travels around the body. This is called blood pressure. It is measured by two numbers, one taken when the heart is pumping hardest (systolic pressure) and the other as the heart pauses before the next beat (diastolic pressure). Measuring blood pressure helps to warn of certain illnesses. If blood pressure is too high or too low, treatment may be necessary.

Donating blood

Sometimes a person loses a lot of blood in an accident or operation. A blood transfusion from another person can replace the loss. It must be the correct group of blood, or it could cause serious problems. Giving or donating blood helps to save people's lives.

DID YOU KNOW?

About 1/12th of your body is blood. In volume, it's about 80 ml for every kilogram of body weight.

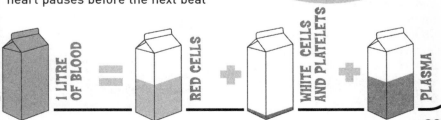

1 LITRE OF BLOOD = RED CELLS + WHITE CELLS AND PLATELETS + PLASMA

23

BLOOD GROUPS
See also Blood, Donors

All blood looks the same, but it isn't. There are several ways or systems of grouping, or typing, blood. The four main blood groups are A, B, O and AB.

Typing and matching
If different types of blood mix, they may form clumps and clots. This could cause problems for badly injured people, or patients having operations, who need top-ups or transfusions of blood. Blood is given by donors and stored in bags. All donated blood is typed to identify its group. Each bag is chosen or matched to a particular patient.

Helpful card
A blood donor card shows a person's blood group. It can help to speed emergency treatment and save life.

Giving blood
Blood donors lie on a bed while blood flows slowly from a vein, usually on the inside of the elbow, through a hypodermic needle and tube into a storage bag or bottle. Blood donors usually give about 470ml during a session.

The procedure takes little time and most people hardly feel a thing. The body naturally makes up the lost blood volume in a few days. After giving blood, donors are advised to rest for a short time before having a drink and a snack.

BLOOD VESSELS
See also Arteries, Blood, Heart and Pulse, Veins

Blood flows around the body in tubes called blood vessels, which form a complicated network supplying every body part. There are three types of blood vessel.

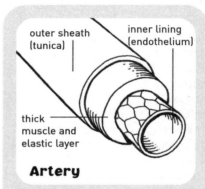

Artery

• Arteries carry blood away from the heart. Their thick walls withstand high-pressure surges of blood from the heart.

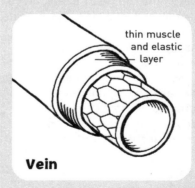

Vein

• Veins, which are wide and thin-walled. They carry blood back to the heart.

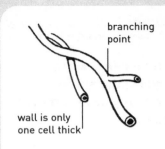

branching point

wall is only one cell thick

Capillary

• Capillaries are far too narrow to see, and usually just 1-2 millimetres long. Capillary walls are so thin that substances such as water, gases and chemicals seep through them between the blood and surrounding tissue.

DID YOU KNOW?

If all the blood vessels from one body were joined end to end they would stretch around the world twice.

BODY ODOUR (BO)
See also Bad Breath, Personal Hygiene, Skin and Touch, Smell

Body odour is a noticeable odour or smell given off by some people. Everybody has some odour, but a few people smell more strongly.

The smell is usually the result of not washing the skin or hair often enough. The odour gets into clothes, so not washing these makes it worse.

What friends are for
A person with body odour often grows used to the smell, and so may not be aware of it. That person may be grateful if a friend tactfully explains about it. The problem is lessened by washing skin, hair and clothes more often, and by using a deodorant.

BOILS
See also Acne, Diabetes, Glands, Skin and Touch, Spots and Skin Marks

Every hair grows from a tiny pit or follicle in the skin. Next to each follicle is a sebaceous gland which makes natural oils and waxes to keep the skin supple. A boil is an infection of the follicle and perhaps the gland with germs, usually Staphylococcus bacteria. Thick yellowish fluid called pus gathers into a head on a red, swollen mound of skin.

Treatment
Some boils gather and burst, while others fade away. While this is happening they can be washed with cotton wool soaked in antiseptic or warm salty water. A sticking plaster helps to stop more germs getting in. Someone who suffers from lots of boils may have an underlying condition such as diabetes, and should have a medical check.

BONES AND SKELETON

See also Accidents and Emergencies, Ankle, Back, Blood, Dislocations, Ears and Hearing, Food and Eating, Hip, Joints, Knee, Neck, Physiotherapy, Shoulder, Tendons, Wrist

Bones are strong, hard and stiff. Together they form the body's inner supporting framework, the skeleton. All 206 bones have scientific names and many have common names – in some cases these are the same.

Most bones have a strong outer layer of or compact bone. It forms a shell around the inner layer, which is light with tiny spaces, known as spongy bone. In the middle is jelly-like bone marrow, which stores fat for energy and makes new cells for blood.

Bones alive!

Living bones are not dry, white and flaky. They are pale grey, with plenty of blood vessels and nerves. They are slightly bendy, so they don't snap easily under stress. They need various minerals in food to stay healthy, especially calcium. Bones are strong in an active body, but weaken if someone is inactive.

What bones do

• **Support**
Bones hold up the body's soft, floppy parts, such as the nerves and guts.

• **Move**
Most bones have muscles joined to them and are linked at bendy joints. Muscles pull the bones and move the body.

• **Protect**
Some bones protect delicate inner parts, such as the ribs around the lungs and the skull around the brain.

• **Store**
Bone marrow stores fat and makes new blood. The bony part contains many minerals which can be used elsewhere in the body in an emergency, such as lack of food.

DID YOU KNOW?

The longest bone is the femur in the thigh. The widest is the pelvis in the hips, and the stirrup bone, which is deep in the ear, is the smallest.

Inside a bone.

periosteum
head end of bone
bone marrow
shaft
blood vessels
compact (dense) bone
spongy (cancellous) bone

Bone problems

If bones are bent too much they fracture or break. The broken parts are put back in their correct positions by a doctor so they can heal, which usually takes two to three months. Unhealthy food and little exercise make bones weaker, so they break more easily. Some older people develop osteoporosis or brittle-bone disease, in which bones become thinner and stiffer.

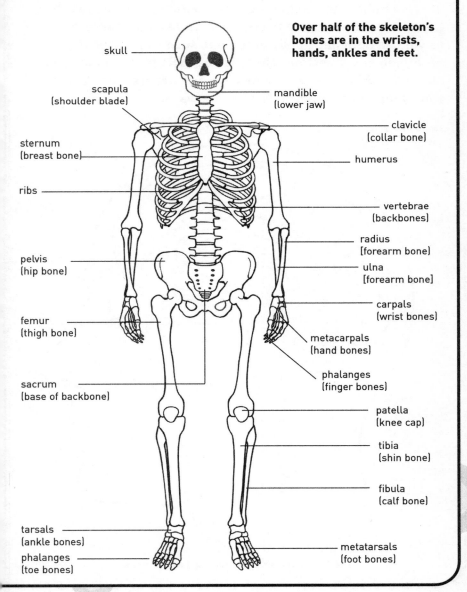

Over half of the skeleton's bones are in the wrists, hands, ankles and feet.

skull

scapula
(shoulder blade)

sternum
(breast bone)

ribs

pelvis
(hip bone)

femur
(thigh bone)

sacrum
(base of backbone)

tarsals
(ankle bones)

phalanges
(toe bones)

mandible
(lower jaw)

clavicle
(collar bone)

humerus

vertebrae
(backbones)

radius
(forearm bone)

ulna
(forearm bone)

carpals
(wrist bones)

metacarpals
(hand bones)

phalanges
(finger bones)

patella
(knee cap)

tibia
(shin bone)

fibula
(calf bone)

metatarsals
(foot bones)

BRAIN AND THINKING

See also ADHD, Autism, Balance, Cerebral Palsy, Depression, Dyslexia, Epilepsy, Fainting, Headaches, Learning Difficulties, Meningitis, Memory, Migraine, Nerves, Psychiatrist, Reflexes, Schizophrenia, Senses, Stroke

The brain is where we have thoughts and ideas, learn and remember, and where we feel emotions, such as fear and happiness. The brain controls our muscles and movements, as well as automatic body processes such as heartbeat, breathing and digestion. There is no single place in the brain where we think or store memories. The brain's many parts work together in amazingly complex ways.

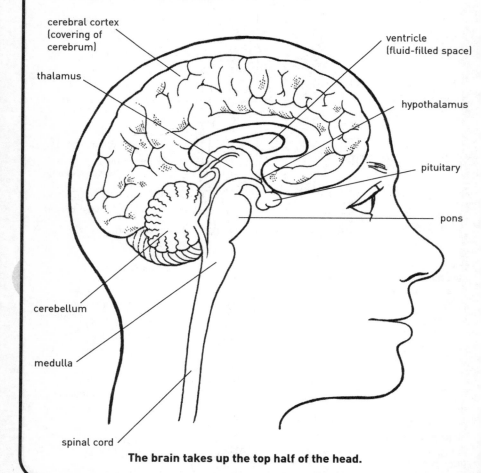

cerebral cortex (covering of cerebrum)

thalamus

ventricle (fluid-filled space)

hypothalamus

pituitary

pons

cerebellum

medulla

spinal cord

The brain takes up the top half of the head.

Size and shape

The brain weighs around 1.4 kilograms and looks like pinky-grey blancmange. It is very delicate but it is well protected by the hard, bony skull. There are more than 100 billion nerve cells in the brain, joined in an immense network like the body's inner internet.

The brain is linked to every body part by nerves which carry messages to and fro as tiny electrical signals called nerve impulses. Every second millions of impulses come into the brain from the senses, and go out to the muscles and glands to tell them what to do.

Upper brain

The big, bulging, wrinkled part on top of the brain is the cerebrum. It's divided into two halves called cerebral hemispheres. The thin grey outer covering of the cerebrum, the cerebral cortex, is where you are aware or conscious of yourself and the world around you, and mostly where you think.

Middle brain

Underneath the back of the cerebrum is a small wrinkled part called the cerebellum. It helps with coordination and the control of muscles, so that your movements are smooth and accurate. In the centre of the brain is the hippocampus, which plays a central role in changing short-term memories into long-term memories, and also the thalamus, which acts like a relay station sorting out messages and deciding which part of the brain they should go to. In the middle of the brain, at the front, is the hypothalamus, the centre for strong feelings and emotions such as hunger, thirst and rage.

Lower brain

At the brain's base is the stalk-shaped brain stem. It contains control centres for breathing, heartbeat, digestion and blood pressure. The lower part of the brain stem narrows into the spinal cord, the body's main nerve, which passes down through the neck and into the body.

EEGs

The brain's tiny electrical impulses pass through the skull to the scalp. Sensor pads stuck on the scalp detect the impulses and feed them to an EEG machine (electro-encephalograph). This displays the signals as a trace of wavy or spiky lines. Changes in the trace help doctors to study brain conditions such as epilepsy and stroke.

WHAT PEOPLE SAY

My brain hurts

The brain feels pain from other body parts, but it does not feel anything in itself – it has no pain sensors. Headaches happen when parts around the brain hurt.

BREASTS

See also Babies and Infants, Birth, Cancers, Puberty

Breasts contain mammary glands which make milk when a woman has a baby. A breast has fatty tissue containing 15-20 groups of glands which produce milk. A tube or duct from each gland leads to the nipple.

A girl's breasts may start to develop any time from the age of nine to 18. Breasts may become larger and more tender just before a period.

Breast problems

Girls and women are advised to check their breasts regularly, for example, each week.

Any changes they notice, such as tenderness, a swelling or a lump should be reported to a doctor. Most lumps are fluid-filled bags called cysts, and the fluid can be sucked out with a needle. Lumps can also be caused by an infection or abscess, which sometimes happen when mothers breastfeed a baby.

Breast cancer is rare in younger women. In the UK women over 50 years are invited for breast screening (X-ray or mammogram) every three years. Breast screening is a method of detecting breast cancer at a very early stage. The sooner cancer is treated, the more successful the result.

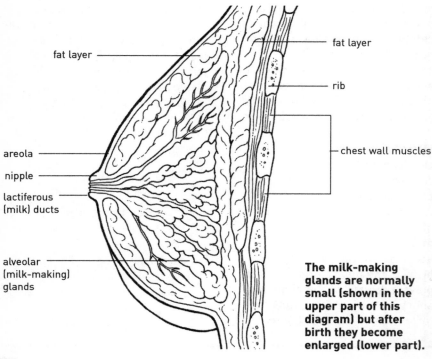

fat layer

fat layer

rib

chest wall muscles

areola

nipple

lactiferous (milk) ducts

alveolar (milk-making) glands

The milk-making glands are normally small (shown in the upper part of this diagram) but after birth they become enlarged (lower part).

BREATHING
See page 97

BRONCHITIS
See also Germs and Infection,
Lungs and Breathing, SARS

Bronchitis is an infection in the bronchi, the main air tubes in the lungs. The linings of the bronchi swell and make fluid, which causes wheezy breathing and coughing. The infection usually comes from breathed-in germs, which may have spread to the chest from a cold or sore throat

Most cases of bronchitis can be cured with rest and antibiotics. People who smoke are much more likely to catch bronchitis.

BRUISES
See also Accidents and Emergencies,
Bleeding, Blood, Blood Vessels

A bruise is caused by blood leaking from blood vessels under the skin. It looks like a red or purple patch which changes colour over days to blue, then perhaps yellow, as the blood is broken down by the body's repair system. Most bruises are small and heal themselves – a cold compress helps to reduce the pain. A large or deep bruise that is still painful after a couple of days needs medical attention.

BURNS
See also Accidents and Emergencies, Skin

Burns can be caused by anything hot, such as a flame, a saucepan, or boiling fat, or by corrosive chemicals such as drain-cleaners. A superficial or surface burn is very painful, while a deeper burn may be less painful but more serious.

Cooling
If the skin isn't broken, cool the burned area with cold running water for 10-15 minutes. If there's no tap, any clean water or a cool item, such as a bag of frozen peas wrapped in a towel, will help. The quicker cooling starts, the better.

Covering
If the skin is broken, cover the burn quickly with a clean dressing or cloth to stop infection. Some first-aid kits have special burns dressings. Whether a burn needs medical help depends on its size, position and depth.

If a burn is small, the casualty should go to a health centre or hospital. If someone has a major burn, phone the emergency services at once and keep the casualty still and covered.

CALORIES
See also Energy, Exercise and Fitness,
Food and Eating, Obesity

The Calorie is a unit of energy formerly used to show the amount of energy in foods. For most scientific uses, Calories (C, which are really kilocalories) have been replaced by another unit of energy, kilojoules (kJ). One Calorie = 4.2 kJ.

CANCERS
See also Cells, Tissues and Organs, Growths, Smoking

Cancer is the general name for a huge group of diseases that affect various body parts. The body's microscopic cells are always multiplying to replace cells that wear out naturally. In cancer, one or a few cells multiply too fast and become out of control. They spread and push out healthy cells, and may form a lump or growth, called a malignant tumour. The cancer can spread to other body parts and affect them too. Benign tumours don't spread like this.

Causes
Some cancers, for example some types of lung cancer, are caused by substances called carcinogens. The chemicals in tobacco smoke are carcinogens.

Other cancers, for example some stomach cancers and cervical cancers, develop as a result of germs such as viruses and bacteria. Some cancers are linked to genes and occur in families. Others are connected to eating an unhealthy diet.

Whatever the cause, cancer treatment is more successful if it starts early. This is why anyone with suspicious symptoms should see a doctor.

Cancer treatments
There are three main treatments or therapies for cancers: chemotherapy, radiotherapy and surgery. These treatments can be used in various combinations.

Chemotherapy
This treatment involves taking powerful anti-cancer drugs, sometimes several at a time in a cocktail. The aim is to kill or disable the fast-dividing cancer cells, while leaving normal body cells unharmed.

Radiotherapy
Radiotherapy uses energy in the form of radiation, such as X-rays or radioactive beams. These are directed very carefully at the cancerous growths, to leave the body parts around undamaged.

Surgery
The third treatment is surgery, to remove malignant lumps. Sometimes apparently healthy body tissues near the growth may also be removed because they may have been invaded by the malignant cells.

CARBOHYDRATES
See also Energy, Exercise and Fitness, Diets and Dieting, Food and Eating, Obesity

Carbohydrates are substances that contain carbon, hydrogen and oxygen. We use this name for foods that contain plenty of starches or sugars used by the body for energy. These foods include pasta, potatoes, rice and bread. You should aim to eat some of these foods at every main meal to maintain a balanced diet.

CARTILAGE
See also Bones and Skeleton, Joints

Cartilage is a tough, light, smooth, slightly springy substance. Articular cartilage covers the ends of bones in a joint. Skeletal cartilage forms the inner framework of the ears, nose and other bendy parts. Cartilage is sometimes called gristle.

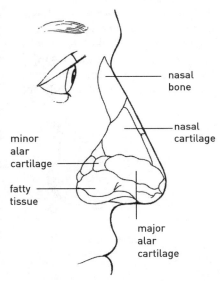

nasal bone

nasal cartilage

minor alar cartilage

fatty tissue

major alar cartilage

The framework of the nose is made of several curved plates of cartilage.

CELLS
See Cells, Tissues and Organs on pages 34–35

CEREBRAL PALSY
See also Brain and Thinking, Fits, Genes and Inheritance, Muscles, Nerves

Palsy is an old word for paralysis – being unable to move properly or at all. Cerebral means to do with the upper part of the brain, the cerebrum. Someone with cerebral palsy is unable to move normally because of a problem in the brain. Babies can have the condition at birth. It may be due to inherited genes that occur in family groups, or to a problem during development of the baby in the womb or during birth. In about three-quarters of cases, the brain's powers of thinking and intelligence are also affected.

Great variety
Cerebral palsy is hugely varied. It may be very mild and hardly noticeable. Or it can be so severe that the child cannot move around or eat without help. But in nearly all cases, the child can be helped with physiotherapy, exercises, and special treatments such as speech training.

CHICKENPOX
See also Germs and Infection, Rashes, Spots and Skin Marks, Viruses

Chickenpox (varicella) is caused by a virus germ, Herpes zoster. It usually affects children and spreads very quickly. Early signs of the infection are fever, pains and feeling sick. A rash appears on the body and face, less often on the arms and legs. Small red itchy spots form which fill with clear fluid. The fluid may turn green or yellow, like pus. Eventually, the spots burst, dry into crusts and fall off. Lotions such as calamine dabbed on the spots help to relieve the itching. The disease usually passes in 7-10 days.

CELLS, TISSUES AND ORGANS

See also Cancers, Doctors, Genes and Inheritance, Heart and Pulse, Lungs and Breathing, Metabolism, Stomach and Digestion

The human body is made up of main parts called organs, such as the heart, brain and stomach. In turn, the organs are made of substances called tissues, such as muscle tissue, nerve tissue and connective tissue. Tissues are made of cells, the body's smallest micro-units or building-blocks.

The human body contains more than 50 million million (50,000,000,000,000) cells. Most cells are so small that about 30 in a row would stretch across this full stop. Cells come in different shapes.

Red blood cells are round like doughnuts, and nerve cells have lots of thin legs like spiders. A cell's shape is linked to its job. Muscle cells are long and thin, like hairs, but become shorter to make the whole muscle contract.

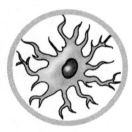

A bone cell (osteocyte) has long branching tentacles that maintain bone tissue around it.

White blood cells can change shape as they squeeze between other cells to kill germs.

A smooth muscle cell is long and tapering. It can become shorter or contract to provide muscle power.

A liver cell is shaped like a box and has a blob-shaped control centre inside, the nucleus.

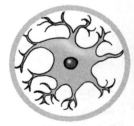

A nerve cell (neuron) has thin wire-like dendrites that link to other nerve cells.

Tissues

A tissue is a group, layer or collection of similar cells. An organ such as the heart has several kinds of tissue. Its outer layer of connective tissue forms a slippery, bag-like container, the pericardium. The main pumping walls of the heart are made of muscle tissue called myocardium. On the inside of this is a layer of epithelial or lining tissue, called endothelium. Inside the heart's chambers is another tissue, which is liquid and flows easily – blood. There are more than 100 different kinds of tissues in the body.

Organs

Organs are main body parts. They are usually made of several different kinds of tissues. The heart, lungs and stomach are organs. The heart pumps blood, the lungs take in oxygen from the air and the stomach digests food. Some organs have several jobs. The liver processes digested food, recycles old blood, stores nutrients such as vitamins, and breaks down harmful substances such as certain drugs.

Structure and workings

Anatomy is studying the structure of body parts and how they fit together. Physiology is the study of how the parts work as they carry out processes such as getting energy from food, making muscles contract, and sending tiny signals along nerves. The thousands of chemical changes which happen in cells, tissues and organs are all together known as metabolism.

Medical research

Doctors and medical scientists study how the body is made and works. This allows them to learn more about living processes, find treatments for illness, detect how the brain thinks, discover how genes work, and do much more to make our lives healthier.

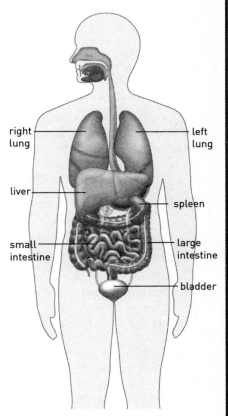

right lung

left lung

liver

spleen

small intestine

large intestine

bladder

The two lungs are the large organs that, with the heart, fill the chest.

CHILBLAINS

See also Blood Vessels, Exposure, Hypothermia

During cold weather the skin turns paler as its blood vessels narrow to save body heat. As the body starts to warm up again chilblains can occur. A chilblain can be a red, itchy, sore patch of skin or a pale, numb area. Children and older people are most likely to have them, on their hands, feet and ears. To prevent chilblains, keep all body parts warm, and avoid scratching, which worsens the sores.

CHOKING

See also Accidents and Emergencies, Babies and Infants, Lungs and Breathing

Someone chokes when the airway in the throat (pharynx) or windpipe (trachea) is blocked. The person gasps for breath, coughs and may turn blue. A severely swollen throat can cause choking, but it usually happens when a lump of food or other item gets stuck.

Choking causes coughing, which should blow out the blockage. If it doesn't, ask the person to breathe in slowly, then cough hard, rather than gasping. If that doesn't work, a first-aider can ask the person to bend over to lower the head, and slap sharply between the shoulder blades in time with the cough. If someone stops breathing, call the emergency services.

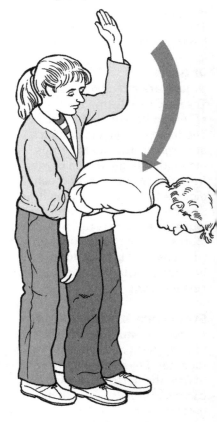

Trained first-aiders can dislodge a stuck item causing choking with a blow between the shoulder blades.

WHAT PEOPLE SAY

It went down the wrong way!

Food goes into the windpipe rather than the gullet if people talk while eating or eat too quickly. This can cause serious choking, or even death.

CHOLESTEROL
See also Diets and Dieting, Fats, Food and Eating

The fatty substance cholesterol is vital for health, especially in the brain, nerves, glands and skin. It is one of the fatty substances needed to make the membrane, or skin, around each microscopic cell of the body. It's also needed to make the insulating covering around nerve cells. But eating a lot of food that is high in cholesterol, such as fatty meats and animal products, is linked to heart disease. This is one of many reasons for eating foods which are low in animal fats.

CHROMOSOMES
See also DNA, Genes and Inheritance

Genes are the instructions for how the body develops, works and maintains itself. They are in the form of a chemical, DNA. In each microscopic cell the genes are packaged as 46 tiny, rod-like structures called chromosomes. These occur in 23 pairs – one of each pair from the mother and one from the father. One pair determines the body's sex. These sex chromosomes are the same, XX, in a girl, but different, XY, in a boy.

CIRCUMCISION
See also Sexual Organs

Male circumcision is the removal of the foreskin over the end of the penis, usually of a baby boy or young child.

When a girl is circumcized, her clitoris is cut off, and sometimes other parts of that area of the body. People usually carry out circumcisions for cultural or traditional reasons. Very few circumcisions are done for medical reasons.

When women have been circumcised they can suffer from sexual, menstrual and psychological problems as a result, and they may have problems and complications when giving birth.

More people are circumcized in some regions of Africa, the Middle East and Asia. It is carried out much less often in North and South America, Europe and Australia.

COLD SORES
See also Viruses

Cold sores are caused by the virus germ Herpes simplex. They are small painful blisters, usually on the lips, mouth and face. Children tend to have them when their resistance is low as a result of another health problem. During the first attack they may also have fever, swollen gums and glands, and feel generally unwell.

Cold sores are very contagious, and a person who has them should take care to use a separate towel and flannel. They usually clear up completely after several days. An anti-viral cream from the doctor can help severe or repeated cases.

COLDS AND COMMON COLD

COLDS AND THE COMMON COLD

See also Bronchitis, Coughs and Coughing, Germs and Infection, Influenza, Nose and Smell, Pneumonia, Sinuses, Sneezing, Viruses

The common cold is caused by one of more than 200 virus germs. The symptoms are a runny, itchy nose and sneezing, a sore throat and cough, watery eyes, a headache, shivers, aches and pains. When you have a cold, your nose may be blocked or full of mucus (snot), which can spread to nearby air spaces or sinuses in the face bones. Gradually the mucus thickens and becomes clogged, and the nose becomes sore from sneezing and blowing.

When you have a cold you should take care not to pinch your nose too hard while blowing it. Otherwise mucus may spread along the connecting tube (the eustachian tube) to the ears.

WHAT PEOPLE SAY

I had terrible flu on Tuesday, but I was fine by Wednesday.
Unlikely! Real flu (influenza) puts most sufferers in bed for several days. Some people feel they've fought off flu but it was probably a mild cold or brief sore throat.

Treatment

Medicines cannot prevent or cure a cold. But ordinary painkillers, breathing vapours or inhalations, rest, keeping warm, and plenty of drinks make you feel better while your body fights the virus. Doctors can do little unless the infection develops into severe coughing, the intense pain of sinusitis, or spreads to the ears. Sinusitis is the swelling, soreness and pain of the linings of the sinuses, which are air spaces in the bones of the front skull and face.

COLOUR VISION DEFECTS

See also Eyes and Seeing

The eye has three main kinds of colour-detecting cone cells, sensing red, green and blue light. Some people are missing one or more types of cone, or have cones that don't work properly. The most common problem is an inability to distinguish between red and green. This colour blindness tends to be inherited and is more common in boys, who can overcome it by learning to distinguish shades rather than colours.

COMPLEMENTARY AND ALTERNATIVE THERAPIES

See also Doctors, Drugs, Hospitals

Most of us experience science-based conventional medicine. But other forms of medicine, known as complementary or alternative therapies (treatments), have been developed. A few of the better known are listed here.

• Acupuncture

An acupuncturist inserts very fine, sharp needles in the skin at specific points, with the aim of helping to improve the body's energy flow. Another alternative therapy called acupressure aims to do the same thing by applying pressure at the same points.

• Homeopathy

A homeopathic remedy is usually a pill which contains a very dilute or weakened substance. This could be a mineral or a herb. The idea behind homeopathy is that a substance that causes certain symptoms in a healthy person can, in a very dilute form, cure similar symptoms in an unhealthy person.

• Herbal medicine

Herbal medicine or herbalism uses herbs and other plant products for their therapeutic or medicinal value.

• Osteopathy and Chiropractic

Chiropractic and osteopathy are used for treating problems associated with bones, joints and the back. Chiropractors focus on the joints of the spine and the nervous system, while osteopaths put emphasis on the joints and the surrounding muscles, tendons and ligaments. Treatment is based on manipulation or forceful handling.

An established complementary therapy, from a fully qualified practitioner, rarely causes harm and may be helpful. But for serious diseases, most doctors advise science-based medicine.

CONJUNCTIVITIS

See also Allergies, Eyes and Seeing, Germs and Infection

Conjunctivitis is an inflammation of the conjunctiva, the eye's front covering. The eyes become red, swollen and painful, and may produce discharge or pus which sticks the eyelids together.

The main causes of conjunctivitis are infection by germs or an allergy such as hay fever. Allergic conjunctivitis can be treated by bathing the eyes with weak saline (salt water) solution or water, but someone with an infection should see a doctor for advice.

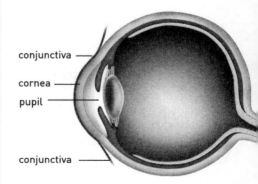

conjunctiva
cornea
pupil
conjunctiva

The conjunctiva is the very thin, sensitive surface layer on the front of the eye. It is washed clean by tear fluid every time you blink. It folds around at the edges to line the inner part of the eyelid.

CONSTIPATION

See also Diets and Dieting, Fibre,
Food and Eating, Stomach and Digestion

Constipation is difficulty in passing solid wastes (stools or poo) or passing them less frequently. It has many causes, from general illness to a change in diet, some drugs, pregnancy, or a problem in the intestines or the nerves controlling them.

Most cases of constipation can be treated simply by drinking water or eating more high-fibre foods. If the problem persists, with fewer than three bowel movements per week, or if there is sudden pain, consult a doctor.

CONTACT LENSES

See also Eyes and Seeing

Contact lenses are small curved pieces of plastic that fit on to the front of the eye, to help it focus for clear sight. Opticians can give advice about choosing and using the best type of lenses for you.

CONTRACEPTION

See also Sex, Sexual Organs, Pregnancy, Periods and Menstrual Cycle, Vagina

Contraception is the prevention of the conception or start of a baby after sex. There are various methods of contraception as shown in the panel on the right.

Some of these methods need a medical check and prescription, and are best discussed with the doctor, partner and – for younger people – caring parents too.

Types of contraception

• **Condom or sheath**
A condom is a very thin piece of rubber which fits over the penis and traps the fluid containing sperm. Using a condom helps to prevent the spread of sexually-transmitted infections. You can buy condoms in supermarkets and chemists.

• **Diaphragm or cap**
A diaphragm is a dome-shaped rubber device that is inserted into the vagina over the entrance to the womb before sex to prevent sperm from entering the womb.

• **IUCD (intra-uterine contraceptive device)**
An IUCD is a wire-like device made of plastic and a metal such as copper. It is placed in the womb to make it difficult for a fertilized egg to grow and start a pregnancy.

• **Spermicide**
Spermicide can be bought as a cream or a jelly. It is put on a diaphragm or cervical cap, or put directly into the vagina. Spermicides all work in the same way by killing sperm.

• **Contraceptive pill**
There are many different types of contraceptive pill. They work in different ways to alter the menstrual cycle so that a woman's ovaries do not produce a ripe egg.

COT DEATH
See also SIDS

A term usually meaning SIDS (Sudden Infant Death Syndrome).

COUGHS AND COUGHING
See also Bronchitis, Colds and the Common Cold, Germs and Infection, Influenza, Pneumonia

A cough is an automatic or reflex action to blast air up from the lungs and clear the throat of dust, fluid or other obstruction. There are many reasons to cough – having a cold or sore throat, breathing in a dusty place or where there are chemical fumes, even feeling nervous. Rarer causes are lung cancer and a lung infection such as bronchitis, when the cough brings up slimy mucus or phlegm.

Croup is a severe cough usually suffered by children, who have noisy breathing and make a crowing sound when gasping for breath. It can come on suddenly at night. The immediate remedy is to relax and concentrate on slow steady breathing, as panic makes it worse. If someone's skin starts to look blue, get medical help at once.

Treatment
Most coughs are useful as they clear the throat and airways. Cough-suppressant medicines may help if a cough is painful, dry, or non-productive (does not bring up mucus). If you have a cough on its own with no obvious cause,

which goes on for several days, it's a good idea to see a doctor.

CRAMP
See also Exercise and Fitness, Muscles, Periods and Menstrual Cycle

Cramp happens when a muscle goes into spasm or contraction by itself, becoming hard, tense and painful. It may happen when the muscle is very active and its blood flow cannot take away the waste product lactic acid. It can also happen if a muscle is squashed, put into an awkward position, used in repetitive movements, or if someone's blood flow is slow, for example, when they are asleep. It may also happen when muscles are used suddenly after long periods of inaction. The main treatment is to stretch and rub the muscle.

Women may have menstrual cramps as part of period pains in the lower abdomen.

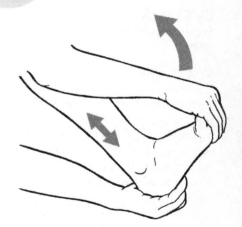

Cramp in the calf muscle can be eased by bending up the ankle and foot to stretch the muscle.

CYSTIC FIBROSIS

See also Genes and Inheritance, Lungs and Breathing, Stomach and Digestion

This is a condition which is inherited and present at birth. It affects the lungs, clogging them up with thick mucus or phlegm, which encourages infections such as bronchitis. It also affects the digestive system. Food cannot be digested properly, so a child with cystic fibrosis is often thin and grows slowly.

There are various medicines and other treatments that greatly help the condition. Tapping the chest while the patient lies with head lowered can help to remove lung mucus. This physiotherapy technique is known as postural drainage.

People who have a family history of cystic fibrosis can consult a genetics expert before having children.

CYSTITIS

See also Bladder, Germs and Infection, Urine

Cystitis is inflammation of the bladder, usually from an infection with germs. Sufferers need to pass urine often and perhaps suddenly (urge incontinence), but only a small amount emerges, and this may smell strange, be cloudy or blood-stained, and cause stinging pain.

Treatment includes drinking lots of fluids, a visit to the doctor for medical drugs such as antibiotics, and great care with cleaning and hygiene after using the toilet.

DANDRUFF

See also Hair, Skin and Touch

Tiny bits of old skin flake off our bodies all the time. Sometimes the scalp produces extra flakes called dandruff, which show among the hairs or on the shoulders (especially on dark clothing). Regular hair-washing with anti-dandruff or medicated shampoo solves the problem.

DEAFNESS

See also Earache, Ears and Hearing, Germs and Infection

There are various types of deafness, from slightly reduced hearing to none at all. The causes range from an ear infection or injury to a baby born with a permanent problem in the inner ear or the nerve to the brain. Ear infections are usually treated easily. Poor hearing after a long-term ear infection may cause learning problems for children, and a medical hearing check is needed. There are many kinds of hearing aids available, including digital versions.

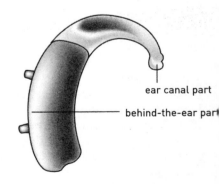

ear canal part

behind-the-ear part

This hearing aid fits behind an ear.

DEMENTIA
See Senility

DENTISTS
See pages 44-45

DEPRESSION
See also Brain and Thinking, Drugs

Everyone gets sad or fed up now and again. It can happen after a serious illness or the death of someone close, breaking up with a partner or best friend, not passing an exam, trouble at school or work or a similar event. For most people the feelings gradually pass and life improves.

Depression is more serious and lasts longer. It may be set off by an event (reactive depression). But in some cases there is no obvious cause (endogenous depression). Depression may also be triggered by a drug, usually non-medical (misused) but in rare instances a medical drug may be the cause.

Signs of depression
A depressed person often bursts into tears for no clear reason, feels worried and anxious, and thinks he or she is a failure and to blame for the world's problems.

Some younger people become withdrawn, avoid joining in with others, and stare into empty space for no reason, while ignoring what is happening around them. They also seem tired and 'flat' and lack any strong feelings – even about subjects such as family, close friends and school. These feelings may be due to a real and serious life problem, which would benefit from being talked about openly. Or they may be due to alterations in the brain and the way its nerve signals and chemicals work.

Treatment
Doctors take great care when deciding if someone is temporarily fed up or suffering from true depression. A firm diagnosis may take some time to make and several doctors may be involved.

There are various forms of treatment. Psychotherapy consists mainly of talking to others about feelings and troubles. Patients visit an expert psychotherapist, or take part in a group, or even talk in a less formal way with supportive and understanding family and friends.

Medical drugs such as anti-depressants are prescribed very carefully because they can have side-effects which may include even more worry and anxiety. Also, some people may become dependent on the drugs, not physically, but mentally.

WHAT PEOPLE SAY

A problem shared is a problem halved.
If we explain our worries to friends and family, they often have a different view. They can help us to see that problems may not be too serious and can usually be solved.

DENTISTS

See also Bad Breath, Gums, Personal Hygiene, Teeth

Most people are advised to visit a dentist half-yearly or yearly. A dentist pokes and prods the teeth, looking for many things – how we clean our teeth, if they are growing well in young people, any injuries or cracks or chips, and early signs of tooth decay.

Oral hygiene includes the health of teeth, gums, tongue and the whole mouth. A dentist or oral hygienist shows you how to use a toothbrush and toothpaste in the right way to clean between teeth and where the teeth meet the gums, and to make sure that all the bits of old food are removed. Brushing is best after meals and last thing at night.

Flossing involves passing a thin cord between the teeth to remove stuck pieces of food. If any old food is left, bacterial germs eat it and make acid, which causes the tooth to rot or decay. Unclean teeth also lead to bad breath.

Good-looking teeth

As baby or milk teeth grow and then fall out, adult or permanent teeth appear in their place. Sometimes these grow slightly crowded or crooked. Orthodontics helps the teeth to grow straight and evenly spaced. Some children need an appliance (brace) to push the teeth into the best position. This may have to stay in place for weeks or months, and might seem annoying, but the result should be good-looking teeth for many years afterwards.

X-rays and fillings

An X-ray shows the inside of a tooth, and whether there are any decayed or cracked parts that can't be seen from the outside. If there is decay, the dentist may drill out the rotten portion and put in a filling substance. This can be silvery amalgam in the back teeth which are less noticeable, or a substance such as ceramic, which is carefully chosen to blend with the tooth colour.

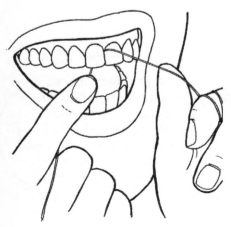

Dental floss is pulled carefully between each pair of teeth with a gentle sawing action.

If small fillings are done early they prevent toothache and the spread of decay which may result in losing whole teeth.

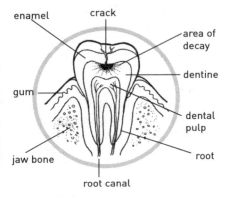

- enamel
- crack
- area of decay
- dentine
- gum
- dental pulp
- jaw bone
- root
- root canal

Decay may look small from outside a tooth, but can be widespread inside.

Crowns

A crown is a false top on the drilled-away lower part or root of a tooth. It can be made of a hard metallic substance containing gold, or a tooth-coloured ceramic.

Results

All parts of the body last longer and work better if we look after them. This certainly applies to teeth. A dentist can help when needed. But with a few minutes' care every day, we can eat and smile with our teeth for almost a lifetime.

DID YOU KNOW?

We have 52 teeth in total. The first set of baby, or deciduous, teeth numbers 20. The second set of adult, or permanent, teeth numbers 32.

Tooth development		
Tooth (front to back)	**Average age baby tooth appears (months)**	**Average age adult tooth appears (years)**
first incisor	6–12	6–8
second incisor	9–15	7–9
canine (eye tooth)	16–34	9–12
first premolar	15–20	10–12
second premolar	24–36	10–12
first molar		6–7
second molar		11–13
third molar (wisdom teeth may never appear)		15–20

DERMATITIS

See also Eczema, Rashes, Skin and Touch, Itching and Scratching

Dermatitis and eczema are very similar, if not the same. Some people use the term dermatitis for a rash, itching or skin redness, which is caused by a substance or chemical touching the skin, such as a household cleaner. Eczema looks the same, but seems to come from within the body.

DIABETES

See also Diets and Dieting, Glands, Hormones, Pancreas

Diabetes mellitus or sugar diabetes is caused by a lack of the hormone insulin, or a problem with how it works. Insulin is made in the pancreas gland behind the stomach and controls the use of glucose sugar in the blood for energy. Lack of insulin causes blood sugar levels to rise, which results in great thirst, the need to urinate often, sugar in urine, weight loss and an extra risk of infections. People who are overweight are at greater risk of diabetes.

IDD

Insulin-dependent diabetes (type 1 or juvenile-onset) usually begins in younger people. It is treated with regular injections of the missing hormone insulin, and by taking care with foods and mealtimes to keep blood sugar levels steady. A diabetic usually carries a card or bracelet with instructions for an emergency.

NIDD

Non-insulin-dependent diabetes (type 2 or maturity-onset) comes on more slowly in older people. It might be found by chance at a check-up. It is also treated by taking care with foods and mealtimes, and perhaps tablets.

Risks

Both types of diabetes can cause problems, for example, with the blood supply to the eyes, feet and other extremities. Doctors, dentists, exercise trainers and others should always be informed about the condition. However people who treat and control their diabetes well can stay healthy and take part in sports and other activities.

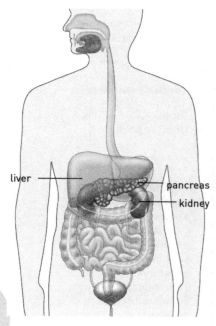

liver · pancreas · kidney

Insulin is made in the pancreas gland in the upper left abdomen.

DIALYSIS
See also Blood, Kidneys

Renal dialysis is the treatment for certain kidney problems. Someone having haemodialysis (blood dialysis) is linked to a dialyzer or artificial kidney machine by tubes. Blood flows to the machine, where it is cleaned and filtered (this is the job your kidneys usually do), and returned to the body. This takes several hours, several times each week.

For peritoneal dialysis a tube or catheter is inserted into the abdomen. Special fluid is passed through the tube to take up wastes, and then drained away some hours later.

DIARRHOEA
See also Constipation, Food and Eating, Food Poisoning, Germs and Infection

Diarrhoea happens when solid wastes (stools or poo) become very loose and runny. There are many causes of diarrhoea: extreme nervousness, illness, a change in food, certain drugs including alcohol, or a problem in the intestines or the nerves controlling them. Common causes are allergy or bowel infection, perhaps from germs in food or drink. This is often called food poisoning.

Treatment
Usually diarrhoea goes after a day or two. It helps to eat a little but drink plenty, for example diluted fruit squash. If the diarrhoea persists, or stools are blood-stained, or if there is sudden pain, consult a doctor. There may be a risk of dehydration from loss of body fluids, salts and minerals, or a serious intestinal problem. This applies especially to babies and toddlers, who need prompt medical attention.

A patient usually undergoes blood dialysis for several hours.

DIETS AND DIETING

See also Anorexia and Bulimia, Carbohydrates, Energy, Exercise and Fitness, Fats, Fibre, Food and Eating, Minerals, Obesity, Proteins, Stomach and Digestion, Weight

Your diet is the food and drink that you regularly consume. But people use the word diet in other ways too. A reducing or slimming diet helps you to lose weight. Some diets are followed for medical reasons, such as a gluten-free diet for someone with coeliac disease. (There is gluten in many everyday foods, including bread.) Other kinds of diets are followed for personal, ethical or religious reasons, such as vegetarian diets.

A balanced diet

A balanced, healthy diet gives your body all the nutrients and energy it needs – and no more. It involves eating:

• Plenty of different and varied foods.

• A wide variety of fresh vegetables and fruits (five or more pieces or portions every day).

• Enough fibre, found in most plant foods, especially wholemeal grains.

• Starchy foods such as rice and pasta (with complex carbohydrates) for energy, rather than cakes and biscuits and other sweet, sugary foods.

• Not too many foods which are high in animal fats or salt, such as fatty and processed meats (burgers, sausuages, salamis and so on).

Any change from this balanced diet, apart for medical reasons, will make your body less healthy.

Reducing and slimming diets

Some people get more energy from their food and drink than their bodies use. The extra energy is changed into body fat. This makes them overweight or obese, which carries many health risks.

The answer to obesity is simple and cheap: eat less food. It also helps to be active and to do more sport or exercise to use up or burn off any excess energy.

Binge dieting

Sudden severe diets, in which someone eats almost nothing for a few weeks then goes back to normal food, do not help the body. Regular eating habits and routines, which result in a slow but steady weight loss, are a better approach. To prevent obesity, a slimming diet should be varied, enjoyable, easily available and not too specialized. Success in losing weight also depends on someone's determination and will power.

Vegetarian diets

Vegetarians do not eat meat or other animal produce. Vegetarian diets are a personal choice – some vegetarians eat fish, others do not. Provided the rest of their diet is varied and well balanced, it should cause no health problems.

Vegan diets

Vegans follow a stricter diet and do not eat any animal products, not even cheese or eggs. Vegan diets must be carefully organized to avoid illness caused by a lack of essential nutrients such as vitamins. Some vegans take these nutrients as extra pills.

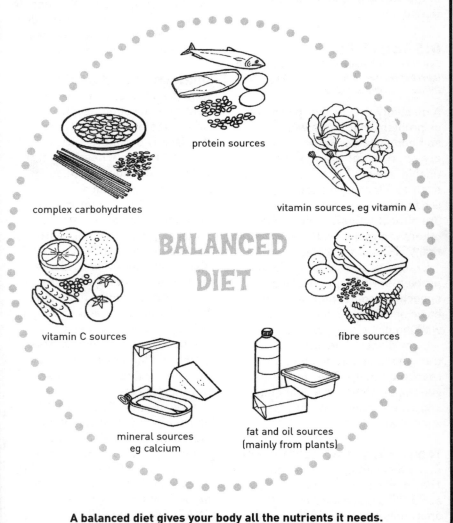

protein sources

complex carbohydrates

vitamin sources, eg vitamin A

BALANCED DIET

vitamin C sources

fibre sources

mineral sources eg calcium

fat and oil sources (mainly from plants)

A balanced diet gives your body all the nutrients it needs.

DIGESTION
See also Food and Eating, Intestines, Stomach and Digestion

When food is digested, it is broken down into tiny pieces, small enough to be used by the body. The process starts with chewing in the mouth, continues in the stomach and finishes in the intestines.

DISABILITIES
See also ADHD, Autism, Dyslexia, Genes and Inheritance, Health Risks, Learning Difficulties, Muscles, Operations

A disability is a loss, impairment or problem that limits what someone can do. Some disabilities are physical, for example being unable to walk. Others are mental, such as a learning disability. Disabilities vary hugely – some are almost unnoticeable, while others are major and affect many areas of daily life.

Examples of disabilities include problems with sight, hearing, speech, learning, memory, and basic activities such as eating, walking or holding items.

Many disabled people have tremendous courage and resourcefulness. They may see the disability as a challenge, and do not want sympathy or special attention.

Temporary and permanent
Some disabilities are temporary. They may be caused by an accident, a disease or an operation. Other disabilities are more long-term – even life-long.

A baby may have disabilities from birth (congenital disabilities), perhaps due to a problem with the development of the foetus in the womb, or to genes inherited from the parents.

A disability may also occur later in life, perhaps as a result of a serious accident that causes paralysis of the legs (being unable to move them). Some non-medical drugs may cause disabilities such as paralysis or memory loss.

Children with disabilities
In the UK almost half a million children and young people (under-16s) have some type of disability or long-term (chronic) illness. These vary from mobility difficulties, such as occasionally needing a wheelchair, to complex mental conditions such as autism.

A large proportion of children with disabilities also have challenging behaviour. This can range from sleeping problems to severe mood swings, damaging their surroundings and self-injury. These problems can have widespread effects on parents, carers and family life, and also affect the child's education and future prospects.

There are many sources of information about disabilities, and the help available, from groups such as Contact a Family, the Council for Disabled Children, the Special Education Consortium, the Special Needs Action Group (SNAG) and Carers UK.

DISLOCATIONS

See also Arthritis, Bones and Skeleton, Hip, Joints, Knee, Ligaments, Sprains, Tendons

A joint dislocates when the ends of its bones move or slip from their ususal positions. This causes pain and swelling; the joint cannot move normally and may look misshapen. A joint has strap-like ligaments which hold the bones in their correct places. A dislocation stretches or tears the ligaments and damages blood vessels, nerves and other parts. The usual cause is a fall or knock. A big dislocation, such as a shoulder, hip or knee, is an emergency. First aid is given to keep the joint and the person still until the emergency services arrive.

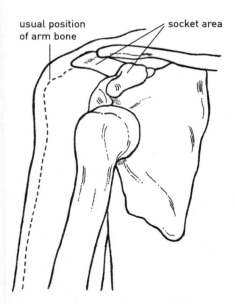

usual position of arm bone

socket area

When a shoulder dislocates the ball-shaped head of the arm bone slips from its socket in the shoulder.

DIZZINESS AND GIDDINESS

See also Balance, Ears and Hearing, Fainting

Someone who is dizzy or giddy may feel light-headed or faint, have problems with balance, and be likely to stumble or fall. They may also have sensations of swimming or floating or feel dazed and confused.

There are many causes of dizziness, from standing up too quickly or lack of food, to a fast theme park ride, looking down from a height, or sudden shock or worry.

Vertigo

A person with vertigo has similar symptoms. They may feel unsteady, unbalanced and perhaps sick (nauseous) and likely to fall over, perhaps due to an infection that affects the balance parts deep in the ear. One example is Meniere's disease, which is thought to be caused by a build-up of fluid inside the balance parts.

The usual remedy for vertigo is to sit or lie down until the feelings pass. If they continue, a medical check may identify a problem such as an ear infection or nerve disorder.

DNA

See also Genes and Inheritance

DNA is de-oxyribonucleic acid, the chemical substance that genes are made of, inside living cells.

DOCTORS

See also Drugs, Health Workers, Hospitals, Operations

A medical doctor is qualified to examine patients, diagnose diseases and illnesses, and suggest treatments. In Britain nearly all medical doctors have the basic qualifications MB BS (bachelor degrees in medicine and surgery) and are registered with the official organization, the General Medical Council. A non-medical meaning of doctor is a person with a higher university or college degree, such as PhD (Doctor of Philosophy).

When people are ill, they first see their family doctor or general practitioner (GP). A GP is both a general doctor and a type of specialist, trained to detect and treat a wide variety of common health problems and ailments. Some GPs have an extra subject or speciality, such as carrying out minor operations. This part of the medical system, involving GPs, practice nurses and other staff at a local health centre, clinic or surgery, is called primary care. If a patient needs more detailed attention, a GP sends or refers

Doctors often check a patient's heart, breathing and blood pressure at the start of an examination.

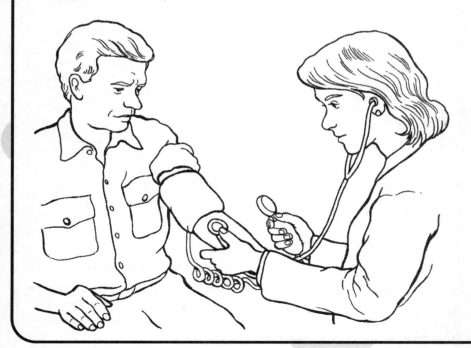

them to secondary care – usually a specialist at a hospital or clinic. Specialists or hospital doctors train in a subject for several years after studying basic medicine. Most begin as juniors, and progress to the more senior roles of registrar and consultant. There are many names for different specialists, often based on the parts of the body or the types of patient they care for.

The doctor's role

A doctor listens to a patient's account of the problem, then may examine the patient. The doctor notes symptoms, which are mainly problems mentioned by the patient, and signs, which the doctor finds on examination. From these, the doctor tries to identify or diagnose the disease, perhaps helped by analysis of samples such as blood or sputum (spit). The doctor then advises treatment or therapy, and may suggest an over-the-counter (non-prescription) medicine or a prescribed medicine. This process and its details are confidential – private between doctor and patient.

Specialists

Anaesthetist – gives anaesthetics to remove pain (local anaesthestic) or to make the patient unconscious (general anaesthetic)

Cardiologist – heart and main blood vessels

Dermatologist – skin, also hair and nails

Gynaecologist – female parts, usually sexual and urinary organs

Geriatrics, Gerontologist – the ageing process and older people

Haematologist – blood and body fluids

Neurologist – nerves and brain

Obstetrician – pregnancy and birth

Oncologist – cancers and similar conditions

Orthopaedic surgeon – bones, joints and the skeleton in general

Paediatrician – care of children and young people

Pathologist – the processes and changes of disease, such as laboratory studies of samples

Psychiatrist – mental and behavioural problems

Radiologist – X-rays and other rays and scans

Thoracic surgeon – chest, especially lungs and airways, also heart

Urologist – urinary system of kidneys, bladder and their tubes

DONORS
See also Blood, Operations

A donor gives or donates something. In medicine this is a part of the body given to help someone else. The most common donation is blood, which is put or transfused into accident victims or people having operations. Some donors are alive, such as a person who donates a kidney. (The human body can function with just one kidney.)

Many donors are people who want parts of their bodies and organs to help others after their death. They carry a donor card or sign a consent form detailing their wishes. Sometimes close relatives of someone who has died may be asked if the person had wanted, when alive, to be a donor.

DOWN'S SYNDROME
See also Cells, Tissues and Organs, Chromosomes, Disabilities, Genes and Inheritance

The body's microscopic cells have their genes packaged as 23 pairs of tiny rod-like chromosomes. People with Down's syndrome have cells which have an extra chromosome – three of number 21. This gives them certain features. Some are physical, affecting their face and body, others are mental traits, for example, being a slow learner.

Some children who are born with Down's syndrome stay well and are able to go to ordinary schools. Others are less able and suffer a variety of health problems such as repeated infections or heart disorders which need treatment.

DREAMS AND DAYDREAMS
See also Epilepsy, Sleep

Most people dream at night. However we rarely remember a dream unless we wake up during it or just after. Dreams happen during light or REM (Rapid Eye Movement) sleep.

When we daydream we spend a short time not concentrating, becoming lost in our imagination. It is often a sign of tiredness. In a few people it could indicate a medical condition such as petit mal epilepsy.

DRUGS
See pages 56–57

DYSLEXIA
See also Brain and Thinking, Disabilities, Learning Difficulties, Memory

Problems with learning to read, write and spell may all be part of dyslexia, which has many different forms. Words may seem to move about, or letters appear reversed (b may be read as d) or transposed (no rather than on). There are phonological difficulties – problems with recognising and sorting the sounds and syllables that make up words. These difficulties may also affect concentration, short-term memory and the ability to deal with numbers.

Causes and effects
The causes of dyslexia are not clear but they are probably based in the way the brain works. Dyslexia may make a young child seem slow or difficult. But the sooner it is identified, the sooner special teaching and activities can start to reduce its effects. Dyslexia may sometimes be passed down through families.

EARS AND HEARING
See pages 58–59

ECZEMA
See also Allergies, Dermatitis, Itching and Scratching, Rashes, Skin and Touch

Eczema is a rash or patches on the skin which can be itchy, dry, cracked, sore, red, scaly, flaking or blistered. Often the patches are at joints such as the elbows and knees.

Dermatitis and eczema are very similar, if not the same. Some people use the term contact dermatitis when the cause of a rash or irritation is a substance or chemical touching the skin. Many cases of eczema may begin with an allergic reaction. Eczema tends to occur mainly in babies and children. Many grow out of it after a few years.

Treatment
It helps to keep skin moist with a lotion or moisturiser, and to resist scratching as this worsens the cracking and soreness. If the eczema is in a certain place and you suspect a contact problem or an allergy, try avoiding the substance that may be the cause, such as a particular soap, detergent scratchy fabric or metal. Prescribed steroid creams and ointments ease the itchy redness of eczema, but must be used carefully because they can have side effects.

ELECTROLYSIS
See also Hair

Electrolysis is a way of removing unwanted hair. Tiny electrical signals from a probe pass into a hair follicle in the skin and through the hair root. The electric current kills the hair, which may not regrow, at least for some time. Hair removal by home electrolysis can work well, but takes time and it's success depends on the user's skill. Professionals usually get better results but cost more.

DRUGS

See also AIDS and HIV, Alcohol, Health Risks, Pregnancy, Tobacco

A drug is any substance that alters the way the body or brain works. The word drug is usually used in two ways: for medicines, which are legal drugs, and for illegal drugs, which can be harmful. A medical drug or medicine helps the body to fight disease and recover from illness.

Some medical drugs are only available on prescription from doctors. Others are non-prescription or OTC (over-the-counter) drugs and can be bought from chemists or pharmacists, supermarkets, corner stores and petrol stations. All drugs are widely tested and continually checked for unwanted side-effects. Users should read the instructions carefully, and ask a pharmacist or doctor about queries or problems. It is important to take the correct dosage and no more.

Non-medical drugs

Illegal drugs, such as cocaine and heroin, are so powerful and dangerous that they are controlled. This means that people are not allowed to make them, take them or sell them except under special conditions with medical permission. Using, possessing or supplying these drugs is a crime which can result in large fines or a prison sentence.

Some medical drugs can also be misused or abused for non-medical reasons, such as getting high or buzzing. (See other pages for drugs such as alcohol and nicotine in tobacco.)

Risks

Taking any drug, even an approved medical one, carries certain risks. Misusing a drug multiplies the risks many times. Taking a home-made drug increases the dangers even more.

Drug misuse

• Side-effects can vary from a skin rash and feeling sick to learning difficulties and permanent brain damage.

• Overdoses can happen if the amount of a drug taken is not known.

• Diseases such as AIDS and hepatitis are spread by unclean injection equipment.

• Injuries and accidents are more likely to happen under the influence of drugs.

• Drug users run the risk of becoming addicted. This happens when the body or mind needs doses of the drug regularly and cannot work properly without it.

• Drugs are expensive and buying supplies can cause great financial difficulties.

Drug use may lead to problems with family and friends, as well as trouble at school or work, and with the police and courts.

Is someone using drugs?

It may be fairly clear if a person starts using drugs. He or she may have odd moods and swings. They may sometimes be very excited but at other times tired, irritable or depressed for no obvious reason. Other signs are lack of money, not taking care with appearance, going missing at odd times, losing interest in day to day events, not making an effort at school or work and hanging round with known drug users. If you think someone you know is using drugs, tell someone you trust, such as a teacher or a qualified drug adviser.

Pressure

No one should feel forced to misuse or abuse drugs. Friends who try to pressurize others to do what they do aren't true friends. A one-off drug experiment might seem a bit of harmless fun, but every year dozens of people who thought that die, become seriously ill or end up permanently disabled.

Fashion

Young people usually rebel and reject what's gone before. They invent their own trends or fashions in clothes, music, hairstyles, cars – and drugs. As new drug cultures evolve, so do fresh risks and dangers. Some drugs are called recreational, making them sound like fun. But the hazards are still there. A new hairstyle can be changed; a criminal record for drug misuse cannot.

Help

There are many sources of help for people who are worried about taking drugs, people who want to stay clear of them, or those who are just curious. These include the website www.recovery.org.uk and the National Drugs Helpline on 0800 77 66 00 (free confidential telephone advice 24/7).

Illegal Class A Drugs

Cocaine (Snow, including Crack Cocaine Rocks, etc)
Ecstasy (E, Whizz, Disco biscuits, etc)
Heroin (Horse, Dragon, etc)
LSD (Lysergic Acid Diethylamide or Acid)
Methadone
Morphine

Opium
Psilocin (Magic Mushrooms – dried or stewed)
Cocoa leaf
Dextromoramide (Palfium)
Dipipanone
Fentanyl
Mescaline
Pethidine

EARS AND HEARING

See also Balance, Deafness, Germs and Infection, Senses

The ears on the side of the head do not hear. The external ear flaps (pinnae) funnel sound waves into a tube called the outer ear canal. The canal leads to a thin, tight piece of skin, the eardrum, which shakes or vibrates as sound waves hit. The eardrum joins to a row of three tiny bones called ossicles, the hammer, anvil and stirrup. These are in the air-filled middle ear space, and carry vibrations to the inner ear.

The inner ear's main part is the snail-shaped, sugar-cube-sized cochlea, behind the eyeball. Vibrations from the stirrup cause ripples in the fluid inside the cochlea. The ripples shake a thin sheet curled into a spiral shape.

This membrane has thousands of microscopic hair cells, each with dozens of hairs sticking up from it into another membrane. As the whole structure shakes, the hair cells make nerve signals, which travel along the auditory nerve to the brain, enabling you to hear.

Damage

Loudness of sound is measured in decibels, dB. A whisper is 10 dB, ordinary talking 50-60, and fairly loud music 70-80. Sounds above 85-90 dB can damage the ear, especially if they are high-pitched and carry on for hours. This is why there are laws controlling the noise in factories, music clubs, sawmills and other noisy places.

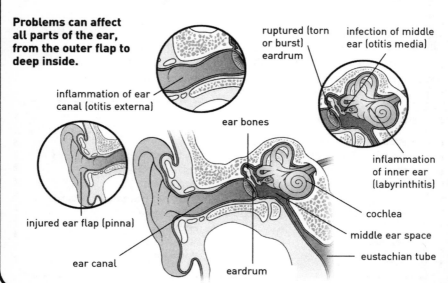

Problems can affect all parts of the ear, from the outer flap to deep inside.

ruptured (torn or burst) eardrum

infection of middle ear (otitis media)

inflammation of ear canal (otitis externa)

ear bones

inflammation of inner ear (labyrinthitis)

injured ear flap (pinna)

cochlea

middle ear space

eustachian tube

ear canal

eardrum

Earache

Pain in the ears has many causes. The most common causes are infections by germs, perhaps after a cold or sore throat spreads to the ears. The pain can be very worrying, especially for babies and young children, who are more at risk of infections. Sometimes young children hit their head or ears in frustration with the pain.

Treatments

Over-the-counter painkillers and a warm pad bandaged to the ear usually help. If the pain carries on for more than a couple of days a doctor's attention is needed. There could be damage to the eardrum or to the delicate balance and hearing parts of the inner ear.

WHAT PEOPLE SAY

I swallowed, my ears went pop and I could hear better.

If you go into a train tunnel, up a mountain or in a plane, the air pressure outside alters and bends the eardrum, limiting its vibrations. When you swallow you open the tube which runs from the throat to the middle ear. This lets the air pressure in the middle ear equalize, so the eardrum works normally again.

EMBRYO
See also Pregnancy

An embryo is a new baby during its very early development in the womb, up to eight weeks after conception.

ENERGY
See also Calories, Carbohydrates, Diets and Dieting, Exercise and Fitness, Food and Eating, Obesity

The body's energy comes from foods, especially starchy and sugary foods or carbohydrates, such as bread, rice and pasta. These are changed into blood sugar (glucose) and used as an energy source for all body processes, from muscle power to thinking. If the body takes in more food energy than it needs, the extra is changed to fat.

All forms of energy, including food energy, are measured in units called kilojoules, kJ. Most adult people need about 8,000 to 12,000 kJ of food energy each day, although this depends on age and activity. Very active people may need twice this amount.

Here are some examples of energy in foods, in kJ:

apple 150–200
banana 250–350
crisps (packet) 600
doughnut 1500
egg (boiled) 500
egg (fried) 800
ice cream (scoop) 600
small sausage (grilled) 500
chicken drumstick (grilled)
   400–550

ENZYMES
See also Cells, Tissues and Organs, Cystic Fibrosis

The human body is a mass of chemical changes, thousands per second. These changes are controlled by enzymes, which are types of body substances called proteins. An enzyme can speed or slow a reaction or change. Digestive enzymes break down food in the stomach and the intestines, and thousands of different enzymes work within cells and tissues.

Some illnesses are due to enzyme problems. People with cystic fibrosis are missing certain digestive enzymes. Some medical drugs block the action of a particular enzyme, or mimic an enzyme to make reactions faster.

EPILEPSY
See also Accidents and Emergencies, Brain and Thinking, Fits, First Aid, Nerves

Epilepsy is a condition of the nervous system. Sometimes nerve cells in the brain fire signals at random, like an electrical storm. This affects thoughts, movements and behaviour, which may result in a fit, seizure or convulsion.

Types of epilepsy

• Minor seizures (or petit mal) can seem like daydreaming. The person stares blankly, does not answer, and may twitch and flutter their eyes.

• A person who has a temporal seizure may seem blank or vacant. He or she may mumble, see or hear things, feel speeded up and carry out strange actions such as rubbing hands.

• A partial seizure includes robot-like actions such as twitching the mouth or thumb, lifting an arm or head turning.

• During a major or general seizure someone may cry out, fall over, go rigid, then twitch or convulse while unconscious.

Treatment
A doctor can prescribe an anti-epilepsy or anti-convulsant drug. Some seizures are prevented by avoiding triggers such as stress, flashing lights, lack of sleep or some foods. People with epilepsy carry a card or bracelet with instructions on what to do if they feel ill or collapse. If someone has a seizure, move away anything dangerous, but do not interfere. Afterwards they can be put into the recovery position or reassured.

EXERCISE
See pages 62–63

EXPOSURE
See also Hypothermia

Exposure to very cold weather is one cause of hypothermia, which occurs when the body's temperature falls very low.

EYES AND SEEING

See also Colour Blindness, Conjunctivitis, Contact Lenses, Senses

For most people, sight is the main sense. More than half the information and knowledge in our brains came through our eyes as pictures, diagrams and words like these. Each eyeball measures about 2.5 cm across, and is well protected in its bony bowl-like socket or orbit.

Light passes through the eye's sensitive clear covering, or conjunctiva, and the dome-like cornea, then through a hole called the pupil, in a ring of coloured muscle, the iris.

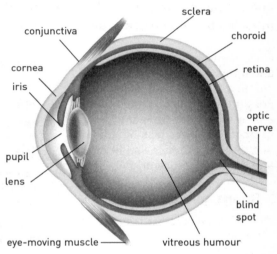

Inside the eye

The iris makes the pupil smaller in bright light, to prevent too much light damaging the eye's interior. Behind the pupil is the pea-shaped lens. It changes shape to bend or focus light rays, becoming thicker for nearby objects and thinner for faraway ones. The rays then shine on to the retina, a very thin layer lining the inner eyeball.

The retina's millions of rod and cone cells make nerve signals when light energy hits them. There are about 120 million rods, which work well in dim light but see only shades of grey. The seven million cones work in bright light and see colours and fine details.

Very clear jelly called vitreous humour fills the main eyeball and gives it shape.

Helping the eye

Some people have eyes which are too big or too small for the focusing power of the lens. So we add an extra lens in front of it, either in spectacle frames as glasses, or sitting on the front of the eye as a contact lens. Regular visits to the optician not only test eyesight. The optician also looks into the eye for any early signs of problems, which can then be treated quickly and more effectively.

EXERCISE AND FITNESS

See also Food and Eating, Diets and Dieting, Energy, Heart and Pulse,
Lungs and Breathing, Muscles, Obesity, Sport, Weight

The human body thrives on exercise and activity. Without movement our joints bend less and stiffen, and our muscles weaken and waste away. Inactive muscles need less oxygen and blood supply, so the heart loses power, lungs become stiffer and cannot stretch so easily to breathe deeply, and the breathing muscles become weaker and tire more quickly.

Movement uses energy from food, and if this energy is not used it is stored as fat, causing weight gain. For all these reasons and more, a body which has little activity or exercise becomes less fit and less healthy. But exercise can fit easily and naturally into your daily life.

Things you can do

• Walk or cycle rather than sitting in a car.

• Choose to walk up stairs rather than using a lift.

• Do physical tasks using your body rather than a machine.

Which exercise?

There are many different types of exercise, from training in the gym and organized sports such as football, to cycling, walking, swimming and jogging.

1 Hold arms out to front then down by sides; repeat 10 times.

What type of activity?

People are more likely to keep up an activity if it is:

• part of daily or weekly routine, rather than at unpredictable times;

• easy to do, without too much specialist equipment or detailed supervision;

• easy to get to, rather than a long journey away;

• not too expensive;

• enjoyable and fun.

How much exercise?

Every body is different and needs different amounts of activity. Any activity that makes you breathless and your heart beat noticeably faster, for more than 20 minutes, two or three times a week, should increase your level of fitness. Compare your latest performance with your previous ones. Aim to improve on your own results every time. If you try to beat someone who is naturally fitter and more athletic, you may get fed up and think of giving up.

Body and mind

Exercise not only improves the body. It can help the mind. Sport or physical activity offers time out from the usual pressures of daily life. You think about different subjects in different ways. Afterwards, your mind feels refreshed and alert. The physical and mental effects of exercise also help you to sleep better.

2 Hold arms above head, lock fingers, then move arms down by sides; repeat 10 times.

Choosing exercise

There are hundreds of activities, exercises and sports. Some people like the social side of team games. Others thrive on competition and beating records. Some like to be indoors, others in the fresh air. Some people like to be on their own, others like company. Choose what suits you best and get out and do it.

Be careful!

• Improve your fitness gradually, over weeks and months rather than days.

• Ease off if you feel dizzy, light-headed, nauseous (sick), or have any pains, especially in the chest.

• Beware of violent actions that may strain muscles.

• Take care when doing the same movement many times.

• Take advice from a trainer or coach.

• Use proper equipment for protection and safety.

• Do warm-up and cool-down routines to avoid sudden stresses and strains.

• Don't carry on if you are very tired, or you may lose concentration and have an accident.

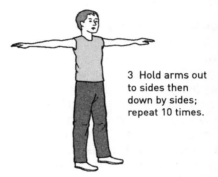

3 Hold arms out to sides then down by sides; repeat 10 times.

Test yourself

Monitor progress by checking your pulse (heartbeat) rate. You can take your pulse rate:

1 Just before each session, at rest.

2 Straight after you finish the exercise.

3 One minute after finishing.

Count the number of pulses in 15 seconds and multiply by four to give heartbeats per minute. Gradually all three readings should come down, especially the important last one, which shows how quickly the heart recovers after activity.

FAINTING
See also Accidents and Emergencies, Brain and Thinking, Heart and Pulse

Fainting is a temporary loss of consciousness due to a lack of blood flow to the brain. The person usually falls to the ground, which brings the head level with the heart and restores the flow of blood to the brain. Fainting is also known as passing out or blacking out.

Causes and treatment
There are dozens of underlying causes, from medical problems such as a heart condition or low blood pressure, to certain drugs, a sudden shock, standing still for too long or becoming very hot. Someone who feels faint should lie down with legs raised, or sit with head lowered. If someone faints for no obvious reason, or is unconscious for more than a minute or two, they should ask for medical advice.

FATS
See also Cholesterol, Diets and Dieting, Food and Eating

The fats and oils in food are greasy, oily or slimy substances, known as lipids. Small amounts are vital for health and are a concentrated source of energy. There are many kinds of fats with different scientific names. Most saturated fats in meats, dairy products and fatty processed food are less healthy than low-fat or plant oil fats (see box on right).

Saturated fats
These raise cholesterol levels and the risk of heart disease. Main sources are:
• Fatty red meats such as pork, beef and lamb, especially processed meat in burgers, hot-dogs, sausages and salamis.
• Some kinds of poultry, including fried chicken.
• Whole-fat dairy products, such as creamy milk, cream, butter, full-fat cheeses and ice-creams.
• Lard and shortening, and cakes and biscuits made using them or butter.

Unsaturated fats
These lower cholesterol and reduce the risk of heart disease. Sources include:
• Most vegetable oils, eg olive, sunflower, safflower and soy oils.
• Oils in nuts, seeds and avocado.
• Sauces and salad dressings made with pure vegetable oils.

FEET
See also Body Odour, Nails, Personal Hygiene

Some feet naturally produce more sweat and odour than others. As with body odour, the owner may not notice the smell, so a quiet word from a friend can be helpful. Foot odour is reduced by washing daily with soap and water, wearing clean socks every day (more often in sweaty conditions), odour-absorber shoe or sock inserts, and shoes dusted inside with anti-odour powder.

FERTILIZATION
See also Pregnancy, Sex, Sexual Organs, Womb

Fertilization happens when an egg cell from a woman joins a sperm cell from a man. This usually occurs in the woman's oviduct (Fallopian or egg tube) about 12-36 hours after sex. However, it can happen outside the body in the fertility test tube treatment IVF, in vitro (in glass) fertilization. The fertilized egg soon divides and starts developing into a baby.

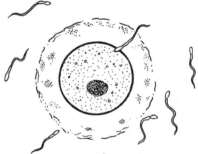

Only one sperm cell can join with or fertilize the huge egg cell.

FEVER
See also Fits, Infections, Temperature, Thermometer

A fever is a raised body temperature, above the normal range of 36.5–37.5°C. This causes flushed skin, which is hot to touch and may be sweaty. At higher temperatures skin may feel dry. Someone with a high temperature may shiver or shake, and feel weak, confused, hot or cold (or both), and thirsty. Sometimes the extra temperature causes a febrile convulsion (fit). A temperature which reads 39–40°C or above

on a thermometer, is serious and needs urgent medical attention.

Treatment
A fever is not an illness but the result of an illness. The main aim is to treat the underlying cause and cool the body. This can be done by removing outer clothes, taking the person to a shady place, and sponging them with cool water. or fanning them. They can also take an over-the-counter medicine such as paracetamol.

FIBRE
See also Food and Eating, Diets and Dieting, Stomach and Digestion

The fibre (roughage) in food is not fully digested and provides little energy. But it is vital to give physical bulk to food to allow it to move through the digestive system. It also helps to prevent digestive problems ranging from constipation to cancer. There is fibre in nuts, vegetables, fruits, cereals and grains (especially wholemeal) and foods made from them, such as bread and pasta.

FINGERS
See also Bones and Skeleton, Dislocations Joints, Nails

We can look after our fingers by wearing gloves for warmth and protection, and by keeping them away from sharp blades and fast machines. A ring should always be removable, in case an injury or illness causes swelling, which might mean the ring would have to be cut off.

FIRST AID

See also Accidents and Emergencies, Bites and Stings, Bleeding, Bruises, Burns, Choking, Fainting, Hypothermia, Sunburn

The three aims of first aid are to save life, stop someone's condition worsening, and to help start recovery. Almost anyone can do minor first aid, such as cleaning and covering a small cut, but procedures such as heart resuscitation should only be carried out by trained people.

If there is a serious accident or if someone has a bad injury, the priority is to phone 999 and ask for an ambulance.

FITS

See also Babies and Infants, Cerebral Palsy, Diabetes, Epilepsy, Fever

A fit (sometimes called a convulsion or seizure) happens when someone loses muscle control and makes jerky, uncoordinated movements. Fits are usually caused by an underlying condition. A febrile fit is the result of high body temperature or fever. Other causes include diabetes and cerebral palsy. Fits which recur may be a sign of epilepsy.

In general, fits are more common in babies and children than adults. Often these are febrile fits caused by an infection such as chickenpox. Some children have one or two unexplained fits and then grow out of them. Anyone who has a first fit should consult a doctor.

FLATULENCE

See also Food and Eating, Food Poisoning, Indigestion, Stomach and Digestion

Flatulence is gas or wind in the digestive system (stomach and guts). It can happen if you swallow air when eating fast, or if you eat foods such as beans which make gas as they are digested. The gas may come out of your mouth as a burp or a belch, or from your anus as a fart (also known as flatus). The old saying 'better out than in' is true. Held-in or trapped gas can cause tummy ache (abdominal pain), so it's best released at a convenient time and place. If gas or wind is a continuing problem, a doctor can advise about medicines and foods to avoid.

FLU

See also Influenza

Flu is the common term for the viral infection influenza.

FOOD

See pages 68–69

FOOD POISONING

See also Allergies, Diarrhoea, Diets and Dieting, Flatulence, Food and Eating, Germs and Infection, Personal Hygiene, Vomiting

The common but non-medical term food poisoning covers many conditions, from food allergy to flatulence (wind). It can occur if a natural ingredient in a food such as mushrooms or berries is toxic or poisonous.

Another cause is germs in food which multiply in the digestive system as a GI (gastro-intestinal) infection. This is more likely to happen if the food is not cooked properly to kill the germs.

The usual symptoms of food poisoning are tummyache (abdominal pain), feeling sick, vomiting and diarrhoea. Most bouts pass in a day or so.

Treatment

The person should sip plenty of water or weak fruit squash as lots of vomiting or diarrhoea may result in a loss of body fluids and minerals. Babies or children with diarrhoea and vomiting need medical attention.

Repeated bouts of diarrhoea, especially if they affect more than one person, may mean a problem with hygiene (for example if people preparing food haven't washed their hands properly), or could be caused by contaminated food.

FRECKLES

See also Melanin, Growths, Skin and Touch, Spots and Skin Marks

Freckles are natural small patches of skin with extra colouring or pigment. They are usually brown, show up on people with fair skin and darken after exposure to sunlight. A freckle that changes for no obvious reason – goes darker, grows bigger, becomes sore, or starts to bleed – should be shown to a doctor in case it is some form of skin growth.

GALL BLADDER

See also Jaundice, Liver and Bile, Stomach and Digestion, Vomiting

The gall bladder (which is different from the urinary bladder) is a small bag under the liver, in the upper right abdomen (tummy). It stores liquid bile made by the liver, before the bile flows along the bile duct into the small intestine, where it helps digestion.

Occasionally hard lumps called gallstones form in the gall bladder. They cause pain and perhaps vomiting and jaundice. They can be treated by medical drugs, ultrasound which breaks the stones into tiny pieces, or an operation.

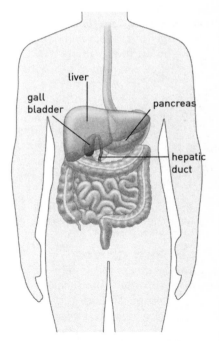

The gall bladder is tucked under the right side of the liver.

67

FOOD AND EATING

See also Anorexia and Bulimia, Carbohydrates, Cholesterol, Diets and Dieting, Energy, Exercise and Fitness, Fats, Fibre, Minerals, Obesity, Proteins, Stomach and Digestion, Vitamins, Weight

Food gives your body the nutrients it needs for growth, maintenance, repair and health, and also the energy to move around and carry out other life processes. Meals can be a rewarding time when you enjoy food, relax and chat with friends or family, but in today's busy world food, cooking and eating are not always high priorities.

Fads, fashions and obsessions

Fashions and trends often affect food and diets. Family members or friends might pressurize us into eating certain foods, or say they taste horrible, when we can make up our own minds. Celebrities are paid to promote the latest diet which may be forgotten in a few months. Some people become so obsessed with having or avoiding one food, that they forget to eat properly. None of this makes much sense. While our brains are in the 21st century, our bodies still have basic stone-age nutritional needs.

Main food groups

Some foods contain many nutrients, others hardly any. It's the proportions of the various nutrients which are important for health, and that is the idea behind a well balanced diet.

Carbohydrates

• Carbohydrates provide energy. They appear as starches in potatoes, rice, bread and pasta, and in cakes, biscuits and chocolate.

Proteins

• Proteins supply building substances for growth and repair. They are in meat, poultry, fish, dairy products, and vegetables such as beans and peas.

Fats

• Fats and oils (lipids) are vital for health and in small amounts for energy. There are many kinds. Saturated fats in animal foods such as red meats, fried foods and processed foods are less healthy than low-fat options.

Vitamins and minerals

• The body needs small amounts of minerals and vitamins to stay healthy, eg iron for healthy blood and vitamin D for strong bones.

Water

• Water is vital. It's good to drink two to three litres or more each day.

Fibre

• Fibre or roughage provides the body with little energy and few nutrients. But it provides bulk to move food through the digestive system. There is fibre in nuts, vegetables, fruit, cereals and grains (especially wholemeal) and foods made from them, such as bread and pasta.

Basic rules for healthy eating

• Eat a variety of foods, not the same every day.

• Have five portions of fruit and vegetables every day.

• Avoid too much fatty food, such as red meat, processed meats such as sausages, full-fat cheeses, crisps, biscuits and cake.

• Avoid adding salt when cooking or eating.

• Try to eat fresh or freshly cooked foods instead of processed meals with additives, preservatives, flavourings, colourings and other chemicals.

• Grill food instead of frying it to reduce fat.

• Try to have three meals daily, including a proper breakfast.

• Put time aside to sit and eat, and make food and eating enjoyable and interesting.

GENES AND INHERITANCE

See also Anaemia, Cells, Tissues and Organs, Chromosomes, Cystic Fibrosis, DNA, Down's Syndrome, Fertilization, Pregnancy

Genes are the instructions for how the body develops, works and maintains itself. They are in the form of a chemical called DNA. There are about 30,000 genes in every microscopic body cell. They are packaged as 23 pairs of thread-like parts called chromosomes. Every time a cell multiplies as part of normal body growth and maintenance, all the genes are copied for the new cells.

Each gene is an instruction for how a body part is made or works. For example, the gene for eye colour controls the colour of the iris in the eye. Several genes work together to determine skin and hair colour, the height of the body, and other physical features. Processes inside the body, such as making enzymes to digest food, are also controlled by genes.

Inheritance

Genes come from parents. Each body cell has two complete sets of genes, one from each parent. When eggs and sperm are made, the double set is halved to one. When an egg and sperm join at fertilization, the double set is restored. We look like our parents because genes are passed on or inherited, although some of our features may be more like our mother and others more like our father.

Dominance

Sometimes one gene of a pair is more powerful (or dominant) than the other. For example, if a baby has a blue eye gene from one parent and a brown eye gene from the other, the brown gene is dominant and so the baby has brown eyes.

Genetic disorders

Some conditions are the result of faulty genes or chromosomes, such as sickle-cell anaemia or cystic fibrosis. These can be passed on from a parent, though it does not always happen. Medical researchers are looking for ways to replace faulty genes inside affected cells. This is known as gene therapy.

Genes are made of the chemical DNA, which has a shape called a double helix.

GERMAN MEASLES
See also Rubella

German measles is an old name for the viral infection known as rubella.

GERMS AND INFECTION
See also Antibiotics, Antiseptics, Bacteria, Food and Eating, Immunity and Immunizations, Personal Hygiene, Viruses, also individual infections

Germs are tiny living things, too small to see except through a microscope. They enter the body and multiply to cause illnesses known as infections. There are hundreds of types of germs, each bringing its own disease. They are divided into four main groups. The smallest are viruses and bacteria, which are described on other pages.

Protist germs
Protists (sometimes called protozoa) are single-celled living things about the same size as a typical cell contained in the body. Most look like blobs of jelly. They usually enter the body in contaminated water, food or drinks. Protist germs include amoebas that cause forms of dysentery, plasmodium which causes malaria, and trypanosome which causes sleeping sickness.

Fungal germs
Fungi include mushrooms, moulds and toadstools. Fungal germs are mainly microscopic yeasts that cause infections such as ringworm and athlete's foot.

Prevention
Germs are almost everywhere – floating in air, in soil and dirt, on surfaces and in foods and drinks. Regular washing, good personal hygiene, avoiding dirt, and covering cuts and sores help to keep them out of the body. So does eating properly cooked food and using treated clean water for washing, cooking and drinking. A healthy body which has plenty of exercise and a balanced diet is more likely to fight off any germs which do enter.

Treatment
Most germs can be killed by substances such as antiseptics (applied to the body) and disinfectants (for general cleaning). Virus infections can be prevented by immunization or jabs. Other germs are killed by specific drugs, such as anti-fungal agents, anti-malarial tablets, and a range of antibiotics against different bacteria.

WHAT PEOPLE SAY

Sometimes our modern world seems so clean, just one little germ can cause an epidemic. Some scientists believe that the body needs to encounter and defeat germs occasionally, to keep its immune defence system working well. This is called the hygiene hypothesis, but it is not clear how true it is.

71

GLANDS

See also Hormones, Lymph Fluid and Glands, Pancreas, Pituitary, Saliva, Sexual Organs, Skin and Touch, Stomach and Digestion, Sweat, Thymus Gland, Thyroid Gland

Glands are parts in the body that make substances, usually liquids, that they release to carry out certain tasks. For example, millions of microscopic sweat glands in the skin make sweat. There are two main types of glands, those which make hormones and those which make other substances.

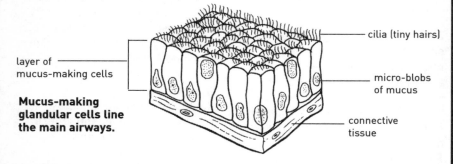

layer of mucus-making cells

Mucus-making glandular cells line the main airways.

cilia (tiny hairs)

micro-blobs of mucus

connective tissue

Non-hormone glands release their products through a tube or duct. Examples include sweat glands, also:

• Sebaceous glands in the skin which make the waxy substance sebum. This natural oil keeps skin supple.

• Six roughly thumb-sized salivary glands in the face make saliva (spit).

• Tiny mucus glands in the linings of the nose, main airways, stomach, intestines and elsewhere make slimy protective mucus. In the nose this is called snot.

• Mammary glands in women's breasts make milk for a baby.

• Sex glands are the ovaries in females and testes in males.

• The pancreas is part of the body's digestive and hormonal systems. It makes hormones and other substances.

My glands were swollen as big as tennis balls!

The glands which swell up during illness, usually in the neck, under the armpits and in the groin, are not true glands. Their proper name is lymph nodes. They are centres where white blood cells fight germs and infection.

GROWING

See also Genes and Inheritance,
Food and Eating, Height, Hormones,
Pituitary, Pregnancy, Puberty, Weight

Every human body grows at its own rate. So comparisons of growth between children of the same age are less important than checking the growth rate of each individual. Some children grow fast early, others catch up later. These differences nearly always even out over time. A very small or tall child may feel awkward when with same-age friends and need support and understanding.

Reasons for increase in body size

• **Genes inherited from parents**
Genes affect final adult height, which is why small stature passes down in families and some ethnic groups, although there are always exceptions.

• **Food and nutrition**
A balanced diet encourages growth and helps the body to reach its full genetic size. Too much food increases weight but not final height.

• **Growth hormone**
This substance, made in the pituitary gland just under the brain, promotes growth during childhood and adolescence.

• **Serious illness**
Some illnesses can slow or stop growth, but the body usually catches up after recovery.

Problems

Growing pains are aches which some children feel when they are aged between five and twelve, usually in their arms and legs. The pains often feel worse at night. They nearly always go away on their own.

Problems with the pituitary gland or growth hormone can speed up or slow down a child's growth, but these are very rare. Blood tests will show if a child has a problem. Problems can almost always be treated, usually by giving the child a series of injections.

DID YOU KNOW?

During your whole life your body grows from a speck-sized fertilized egg into a fully developed adult. That's a weight increase of about nine billion times!

GROWTHS

See also Cancer

This term usually means some sort of lumpy new tissue which may be a relatively harmless cyst or ganglion, or a tumour which can be benign (non-cancerous) or malignant (cancerous). The exact type of growth may be identified by taking a sample of it (biopsy) for laboratory tests. Non-serious small growths may be left unless they cause trouble.

GULLET

See also Heartburn, Stomach and Digestion, Vomiting

The gullet or oesophagus carries swallowed food from the throat down through the neck and chest to the stomach. It is sometimes called the foodpipe.

Food does not fall down the gullet, but is pushed down by the wave-like squeezing of the strong muscles in the gullet wall. These waves work the other way to bring food up from the stomach when you vomit (are sick or throw up).

Any pain or difficulty in swallowing should be reported promptly to a doctor. Usually the problem is muscle strain or soreness. But if the cause is more serious, the sooner it's treated, the better.

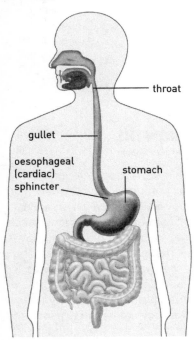

throat

gullet

oesophageal (cardiac) sphincter

stomach

GUMS

See also Cold Sores, Dentists, Teeth, Ulcers

The gums or gingivae are the pink coverings of the jawbones around teeth that help to keep your teeth in place. Swollen, sore or bleeding gums are signs of gingivitis, a mild form of gum disease. It can be prevented by brushing and flossing teeth properly and by rinsing with mouthwash at least once each day. Painful gums or ulcers are best reported first to a dentist or dental (oral) hygienist rather than a doctor.

HAEMOPHILIA

See also Bleeding, Blood, Genes and Inheritance

Haemophilia is a genetic condition in which blood does not clot properly, so it continues to leak from a cut or bruise. Haemophilia is the result of a missing chemical, factor VIII (8), which is part of the complicated blood clotting (coagulation) process.

People with haemophilia take extra care to prevent injury, for example, by avoiding contact sports. They may need injections of the missing chemical. If haemophilia runs in a family, a doctor or genetic counsellor can advise on the risk of passing the condition to children.

The gullet is a strong, muscular tube about 25 cm long, going from the bottom of the throat to the stomach.

HAIR

See also Dandruff, Melanin, Nails, Skin, Personal Hygiene

We have millions of hairs all over our bodies, but most are so small we don't notice them. When we think of hair we think of the 100,000 or so hairs on our head. Each hair grows from a tiny pocket-like pit in the skin called a follicle.

The hair lengthens at its base or root and pushes out of the skin. The rod of microscopic cells which form the hair fill with the tough substance keratin, which also makes up the outer layer of skin. Hair cells die by the time they are level with the skin's surface. So a hair itself cannot feel anything (otherwise a haircut would hurt). Sensations of pain come from the nerve ends around the follicle.

Every scalp hair grows about three millimetres per week for a few years, then falls out. A new hair sprouts from the empty follicle. This happens all over the scalp at different times, so a comb or hairbrush usually has up to 100 hairs in it.

Colours and types

Hair colour and type – straight, wavy, curly – is mainly under the control of the genes inherited from your parents. You can cut, dye and style your hair but it will always grow back with its natural colour and type.

Hair care

Hair needs washing every two or three days, but this depends on the individual. Some people have oily hair while others have dry and brittle hair. Conditioners and other treatments may help hair to look soft and shiny. Daily combing or brushing keeps away knots, tangles and bits of dirt.

- hair shaft
- epidermis
- sebaceous gland
- dermis
- hair follicle
- hair root

A hair follicle is a pocket-like pit in the lower layer of skin, the dermis.

WHAT PEOPLE SAY

Eating sprouts or crusts will make your hair curl.
No it won't. But eating a healthy, balanced diet helps hair grow well.

HANDS
See also Fingers, Nails, Skin, Tendons

We use our hands almost every minute of the day. So they need good care and protection. Gloves stop hands getting too cold, which can make them feel numb and unable to move or grip properly. This increases the risk of accident and injury. Gloves also protect hands from wear and friction, and the danger of machines or tools. Constant rubbing or pressure makes the skin grow thicker forming a hard pad or callus. This usually fades away when the rubbing stops.

Finger muscles
Most of the muscles that move the fingers are in the forearm and linked to the fingers by long tendons that run through the wrist. If you look at the inside of your forearm and clench your fingers hard into a fist you can see the muscles tense and the tendons tighten in your wrist.

HAY FEVER
See also Allergies, Eyes and Seeing

Hay fever is the body's reaction to normally harmless pollen – the tiny dust-like specks or grains produced by plants. Some people are allergic to hay or grass pollen, others to tree or flower pollen. Symptoms are itchy, runny, red, sore eyes, also an itchy and runny nose, sneezing, and a tickly throat. Hay fever is also called seasonal allergic rhinitis. It's worth trying several anti-histamine medicines

Self-help and treatment

• Stay indoors if possible in the worst weeks to avoid the pollen-laden air outside, especially on windy days.

• Wash hair and pillowcases often. Pollen sticks to hair and gets on to pillows, causing symptoms at night.

• Wear sunglasses to protect the eyes from pollen and because bright sunshine worsens eye irritation.

• Bathe eyes with eye-cleansing lotion to remove pollen and ease soreness.

to find the most effective one for you, since people react differently to them. In a treatment called desensitization the sufferer receives injections monthly, perhaps continuing over a few years, but results are far from guaranteed.

HEADACHES
See also Brain and Thinking, Meningitis, Migraine, Sinuses, Tiredness

A headache isn't an illness, but the result of an underlying problem – from simple tiredness to a serious brain tumour.

Headaches are common during infections, and even a common cold can trigger a headache. Lack of sleep or a different routine, for example working night-shifts or travelling long distances, can also cause them. So can worry and stress. In most cases the ache fades when the cause does. A headache that continues for more than a day, making it difficult to carry on with normal life, should receive medical attention.

Certain kinds of severe repeated headaches are called migraine.

Further causes of headaches

• A knock on the head. If the brain swells or bleeds (haemorrhage), a headache may not occur until hours or days later. Anyone who faints after a head injury needs a medical check.

• Meningitis. Other symptoms of this illness include a stiff neck, eye pain when exposed to bright lights and skin rash.

• Sinusitis, which is swelling in the sinuses (air spaces) in the bones of the face. Pain is usually felt above the eyes or at the sides of the nose.

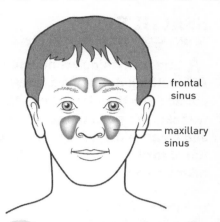

frontal sinus

maxillary sinus

The pain of sinusitis comes from air spaces within the skull bones of the face.

HEALTH RISKS
See pages 78-79

HEALTH WORKERS
See also Doctors and Nurses, Dentists, Physiotherapists, Radiotherapy

There are many job titles for people who work in the health service. Here are a few examples:

• Health visitors come to people's houses, especially to visit mothers with young babies.

• Physiotherapists specialize in movement and exercise, particularly for muscle and joint problems.

• Radiotherapists take X-rays, scans and similar pictures.

• Occupational therapists help people to recover from a long or serious illness such as a stroke.

WHAT PEOPLE SAY

My headache's so bad, my skull will split!
No way! The skull is far too strong. But if the brain swells due to injury or infection, it pushes against the inside of the skull and puts pressure on itself.

HEALTH RISKS

See also AIDS and HIV, Diets and Dieting, Drugs, Food and Eating, Obesity, Sex, Tobacco

Almost anything we do might be a health risk.
Walking downstairs, travelling in a car, eating a pizza, going outside in a thunderstorm – there are hazards in every action we take. We need to recognize risks when we encounter them, and balance the need for sensible care and caution against the fun of thrills and excitement, which come from occasionally taking a chance.

Think about the situations above. Which harms fewest people: stairs, cars, pizzas or thunderstorms? The answer is thunderstorms. Most people are wary of thunder and lightning because they are quite rare and have the reputation of danger. So when there is thunder and lightning we take care to stay safe. But we might fall down stairs, be injured in a car accident, or choke while rushing to eat food. If hazards are around us every day, we get used to them, so we may forget to take proper care.

Major health risks

The main health risks which we can influence by our choices and lifestyle include:

• **Smoking tobacco**
This is a massive cause of illness and death, as well as being expensive, smelly, very annoying to some people, and increasingly outlawed in workplaces and public spaces such as theatres, bars and shopping centres.

• **Taking non-medical drugs**
These include drinking alcohol and inhaling solvents. They may seem fun, but every day people suffer sickness, accidents, problems at school or work, arguments with family and friends, money difficulties and perhaps trouble with the law.

• **Dangerous activities**
Organized activities such as skydiving or horseriding can give a real thrill or buzz, yet the risks are kept to a minimum by proper equipment, training and supervision. Far more hazardous are dare games such as motorway chicken or train surfing, in which people run the risk of being killed and leaving behind devastated family and friends.

• **Obesity**
Being overweight increases the risks of many conditions and diseases, from diabetes and heart problems to arthritic joints and even certain cancers.

- **Unhealthy food**
The wrong type of diet can lead to many illnesses including heart attacks and cancers.

- **Unprotected sex**
This can pass on several kinds of serious infections including HIV/AIDS, or have the side effect of an unwanted pregnancy.

Everyday risks

Most hazards to health are in familiar situations such as homes, workplaces, local roads, and in cars, on bikes or messing about. Also most victims of violence or abuse suffer at the hands of someone they know. It's hard to stay constantly aware of all this in daily life, but following a few simple life rules helps. For example, try to cross the road at a pedestrian crossing, wear a cycle helmet when out biking and always say no to suspicious suggestions.

The right to choose

Sometimes it's difficult to make the right choice and avoid a health risk, especially on the spur of the moment. Friends or people we admire might encourage us to take risks that we know are wrong. 'Go on, just try this once, it won't hurt.' But it might. True friends respect our decisions and do not put us under too much pressure. Also, if we take health risks and something goes wrong, resulting in injury or illness, this affects people around us.

Health and other parts of our lives

There are obvious health risks, such as smoking and taking drugs. There are also parts of our lives which are linked to staying healthy, but which may not seem to be. Some of these we can change; others we can't. But it can help if we are aware of how they affect us and the way we see health risks.

- Some people simply don't take care of themselves, or think their own health is important, and this can rub off on others.

- Some people just like to take lots of risks – at school, with the law, by teasing friends or with their own well-being. They drag others along into illness and injury.

- Our experiences as children have huge effects on how we view our own health: whether we come from city or country, if we are rich or poor, our cultural background, ethnic group, religion or faith.

- Modern media, such as TV soaps, magazines and internet sites also shape our ideas about risks to our own health.

HEARING
See also Deafness, Ears and Hearing

The sense of hearing detects invisible sound waves which pass through the air to our ears.

HEART
See pages 82–83

HEARTBURN
See also Food and Eating, Gullet, Hernias, Indigestion, Obesity, Stomach and Digestion

Heartburn is a form of indigestion; it has nothing to do with the heart. It feels like a hot or burning pain in the chest and throat. Heartburn happens when the acid juices in the stomach well up into the lower gullet (oesophagus). It tends to occur after large meals of fatty or spicy foods, and too much alcohol.

Most people suffer from heartburn at one time or another, but overweight people, and people with a hiatus hernia are particularly at risk. Heartburn can be treated with antacid (anti-acid) indigestion remedies.

HEPATITIS
See also Jaundice, Liver and Bile, Tattoos, Viruses

Hepatitis is the swelling and inflammation of the liver. It is caused by various viruses, usually known as hepatitis A, B, C, D and E. The viruses are spread by contaminated water or food, or poor hygiene (A and E), by blood contact, for example from unclean needles used for drug injection, or during sex (B, C and D). People at risk, such as health workers, can be immunized or vaccinated against some forms.

Effects
Most types of hepatitis begin with a headache and raised temperature, followed by vomiting, digestive upsets and jaundice (yellowing of the skin and eyes). Treatment involves mainly rest and diet, with medical drugs in rare cases.

HERNIAS
See also Muscles, Heartburn

A hernia is an inner body part which pokes though its covering or container (usually a sheet of muscle) and shows as a lump under the skin. Most hernias occur around the abdomen. An inguinal hernia is in the groin area. A hiatus hernia happens when part of the stomach slips up through the diaphragm (main breathing muscle) into the chest. Some babies have an umbilical hernia in the navel (tummy-button) area. The usual treatment for most hernias is an operation.

HERPES
See also Chickenpox, Cold Sores, Germs and Infection, Shingles, Viruses

Types of Herpes viral germs cause infections such as cold sores around the mouth, the rash and spots of chickenpox, and the painful nerve problem called shingles.

HEART AND PULSE

See also Blood, Blood Vessels, Exercise and Fitness, Heart Attacks,
Hormones, Lungs, Oxygen

Between the lungs in the chest, slightly to the left side,
is the body's busiest part – the heart. It is a muscular
bag that pumps once every second, all through your life,
to push blood around the set of tubes called blood vessels.
Your heart is about the size of your clenched fist.

Inside, the heart is not one
pump but two, side by side.
The right pump sends blood
to the lungs to collect fresh
supplies of oxygen. This blood
returns to the heart's left side,
which pumps it around the body
to supply oxygen to all the
working parts. The blood comes
back to the heart's right side and
so the journey, or circulation,
continues round and round.

Inside the heart

Both sides of the heart have
two hollow parts or chambers.
The upper atrium is small, thin-
walled and floppy, and blood flows
into it from the veins. The blood
passes through a one-way valve
into the lower chamber or
ventricle, which is larger with
walls of thick muscle. During
a heartbeat, each ventricle
squeezes powerfully to force
the blood out through another
one-way valve into the arteries.

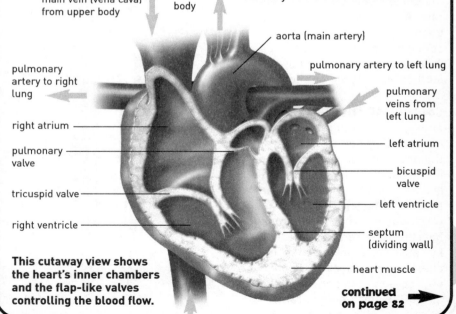

main vein (vena cava)
from upper body

to upper body

aorta (main artery)

pulmonary artery to right lung

pulmonary artery to left lung

pulmonary veins from left lung

right atrium

left atrium

pulmonary valve

bicuspid valve

tricuspid valve

left ventricle

right ventricle

septum (dividing wall)

heart muscle

from lower body

**This cutaway view shows
the heart's inner chambers
and the flap-like valves
controlling the blood flow.**

**continued
on page 82** ➡

HEART AND PULSE continued

Heart muscle

The heart muscle is called myocardium, and it never tires. It has its own blood supply from vessels called coronary arteries and veins, which branch over its surface. The heart is wrapped in a slippery bag, called the pericardium. This allows it to squirm easily and smoothly inside the chest with every beat.

Heart rate and pulse

When the body rests, the heart pumps about 60-70 times per minute – faster in younger people. When the body is active, the beat speeds up. We can feel the force of the blood pushed out of the heart as a bulge in the artery in the wrist – the pulse. Counting the pulse gives the heart's beating rate. As the valves in the heart open and close they make the sound of a heartbeat: lub-dup. A doctor hears this through a stethoscope placed on the chest.

Control of the heart

The heart's beating rate is controlled by nerve signals from the brain, and also by hormones in the blood. The main hormone is adrenaline, which makes the heart beat faster. Tiny bursts of electricity made by the pumping heart muscle can be picked up by sensor pads (electrodes) on the chest and displayed as a spiky line on a screen or paper tape called an ECG (electro-cardiogram).

The heart is the pump for the circulatory system which carries blood all around the body.

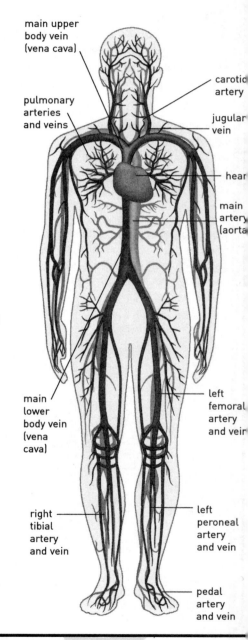

main upper body vein (vena cava)

carotid artery

pulmonary arteries and veins

jugular vein

heart

main artery (aorta)

main lower body vein (vena cava)

left femoral artery and vein

right tibial artery and vein

left peroneal artery and vein

pedal artery and vein

Heart attacks

Heart attack is the common term for a sudden or acute heart problem. Most often it describes coronary thrombosis, which happens when a blood clot (thrombosis) blocks one of the coronary arteries supplying blood to the muscular walls of the heart. Other causes of heart attack include a problem with the electrical signals that tell the heart muscle to contract.

CT and MI

Coronary thrombosis occurs when the arteries are narrowed by lumps or deposits of fatty substance in their inner walls. This condition, coronary heart disease, is the result of several factors including being male, being older, smoking, not taking exercise and having a high level of cholesterol in the blood.

The clot blocks blood flow to the heart muscle, or myocardium. The muscle begins to die due to lack of oxygen, known as infarction. So coronary thrombosis (CT) leads to myocardial infarction (MI), which disrupts the heart's vital pumping action.

Cardiac arrest

Cardiac (heart) arrest happens when the heart stops beating. The cause may be coronary thrombosis or a problem of heart rhythm, such as fibrillation, when different parts of the heart muscle twitch without coordination.

Signs and treatment

A heart attack victim usually looks pale and sweaty, feels ill and breathless, and has a vice-like gripping pain in the chest which may extend along the left shoulder and arm. Emergency help should be summoned immediately (a paramedic or ambulance) and the victim should lie still and stay calm.

Heart murmurs

The heart makes a lub-dup sound with every beat. Doctors listen carefully through a stethoscope for anything out of the ordinary in this sound, especially in the heatbeats of babies and children. An unusual heart sound, such as rustling or unevenness, may be called a murmur. Sometimes there is no underlying problem. In other cases further tests may be done to check the heart valves which make the sound.

WHAT PEOPLE SAY

My heart was full of love.
Strong feelings and emotions happen in the brain, not the heart. But powerful emotions can make the brain tell the heart to pump faster or flutter.

HICCUPS (HICCOUGHS)

See also Lungs and Breathing

Most people get hiccups when they have been eating and drinking and have a very full stomach. This causes the stomach to bulge up against the dome-shaped main breathing muscle, the diaphragm. The pressure irritates the muscle or squeezes the nerve controlling it. This makes the diaphragm tense or contract suddenly at random, causing a jerky intake of breath when the vocal cords snap together with a hic.

Certain drugs can make hiccups more likely, including alcohol, and being overweight can increase the risk or the time they last.

Remedies

Most attacks of hiccups fade on their own. There are many kinds of treatments and cures, for example:

- **Holding breath for as long as possible.**

- **Singing a song while trying to breathe in.**

- **Sipping water from the opposite or far side of a cup or glass.**

- **A sudden distraction or fright – BOO!**

If hiccups last more than 30–60 minutes and seem to have no cause, inform a doctor. In very rare cases there may be an underlying problem.

HIP

See also Bones and Skeleton, Dislocations, Joints

The hip is a ball-and-socket joint. The hip region has the largest bone, the hip bone or pelvis, and the second-biggest joint after the knee. Some babies are born with CDH, congenital dislocation of the hip. This happens when the ball-shaped upper end or head of the thigh bone slips or dislocates easily from its socket in the hip bone. It can be treated by strapping and manipulation, and perhaps an operation.

A broken hip is usually a break at the upper end of the thigh bone or femur. A broken or dislocated hip is a medical emergency.

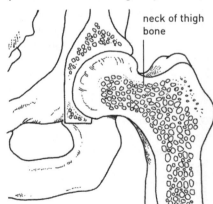

neck of thigh bone

A broken hip often occurs at the neck of the thigh bone.

HIV

See also AIDS and HIV

Human Immunodeficiency Virus, HIV, is the viral germ that causes the condition of AIDS.

HORMONES

See also Adrenaline and Adrenal Glands, Diabetes, Glands, Growing, Metabolism, Pancreas, Pituitary, Puberty, Sexual Organs, Thyroid Gland

Hormones are natural chemical substances that travel around the body in the blood and affect the way it works. They are made in the hormonal or endocrine glands. Hormones, along with the brain and nerve system, control and coordinate many body processes. Some hormones affect just one or two body parts, called the target organs. Others affect the whole body. The main hormonal glands are also covered on other pages.

Pituitary

This pea-sized hormonal gland under the brain produces several hormones that control major processes such as growth and sexual development, as well as hormones that control other hormonal glands.

Thyroid

The thyroid gland in the neck produces thyroxine, which speeds up chemical changes and energy use in the body.

Parathyroids

Four tiny glands embedded in the thyroid make parathormone to regulate the mineral calcium in the blood.

Pancreas

The pancreas is both a digestive and hormonal gland. Its two main hormones are insulin and glucagon, which control how the body's microscopic cells use glucose (blood sugar) for energy.

Adrenals

The adrenals make hormones to help fight stress and illness, and regulate fluid balance and urine production. Their best known hormone, adrenaline, prepares the body for fast action.

Body parts such as the stomach and kidneys make hormones in addition to their main tasks. Hormonal problems such as diabetes are identified from symptoms and measurements of the hormone in the blood. Most can be treated by tablets or injections.

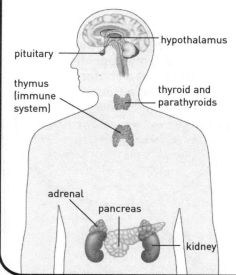

pituitary

hypothalamus

thymus (immune system)

thyroid and parathyroids

adrenal

pancreas

kidney

HOSPITALS

See also Doctors and Nurses, Health Workers, Operations

Hospitals are places where people are treated for diseases, illnesses, accidental injury and other health problems. A general or district hospital provides most kinds of treatments. Specialist hospitals deal with only some areas of medicine, such as cardiology (heart), neurology (brain and nerves) or maternity (mothers and babies). Any of these can also be teaching hospitals to train doctors. Local and cottage hospitals are smaller and cope with less serious illnesses.

Departments

A large hospital has thousands of staff who work in many departments, from non-medical security, catering and cleaning, to surgical operating theatres, ICUs (Intensive Care Units for very ill people), A&E (Accident and Emergency or Casualty), Oncology (specialized cancer care) and general wards. Diagnostic departments include X-ray and Imaging (Radiology), and Pathology laboratories for testing blood and other samples. There are also therapeutic or treatment departments such as Physiotherapy.

Out and in

Out-patient clinics and day centres do not involve overnight stays. In-patients are admitted to stay for one or more nights. When they are well enough they are discharged from hospital and can go home, or stay with relatives or at a convalescent centre. They may need to return or visit their family doctor for follow-up appointments.

Doctors

Most hospital doctors begin as juniors or trainees, then progress through various levels of registrar to the more senior role of consultant. Some become specialists; others prefer general medicine. There are many names for specialists, usually based on the parts of the body or types of patients they care for (see page 53).

WHAT PEOPLE SAY

I hope he's not doing my operation. He's just a Mister, not even a Doctor!
Male surgeons are known as Mister, although they have more training than many doctors and the letters FRCS (Fellow of the Royal College of Surgeons) after their names.

HYPOTHERMIA

See also Accidents and Emergencies, Chilblains, Exposure, Fever, Temperature, Thermometer

Hypothermia is a dangerous fall in body temperature to below about 35°C. Causes include being outside in winter (exposure), being inside without proper heating or clothes, or falling into cold water. Someone with hypothermia becomes pale, confused and weak and may lose consciousness. He or she should be given emergency help as soon as possible. Prevent further cooling, but rewarming is best left to experts, as if it is done too quickly it may cause further problems.

A person suffering from hypothermia feels cold to the touch and should be well wrapped.

IMMUNITY

See page 88

INCONTINENCE

See also Constipation, Diarrhoea, Kidneys, Stomach and Intestines, Urine

Incontinence is the leakage of urine (wee) or faeces (poo) out of the body at the wrong time. There are many causes, from a sudden violent cough or an emotional shock, to a disease that affects the nerves or muscles.

Treatment depends on the cause and includes special exercises, wearing underwear with liners or pads, medical drugs and rarely, an operation.

INDIGESTION

See also Appendix, Constipation, Diarrhoea, Flatulence, Food and Eating, Food Poisoning, Stomach and Digestion, Vomiting, Wind

Indigestion is the term used for discomfort or pain in the abdomen (lower body). It is usually caused by digestive problems which can range from eating too fast or having trapped wind to a stomach ulcer, food poisoning or appendicitis. Some food allergies can also cause indigestion, which is known as abdominal discomfort or distension. Most people recover from indigestion in a day or two, perhaps with medicine from the chemist. If the problem continues for longer, or is accompanied by vomiting and diarrhoea, or becomes so severe that the sufferer doubles up in pain, urgent medical help is needed.

IMMUNITY AND IMMUNIZATIONS

See also Antibodies, BCG, Diphtheria, Germs and Infection, Hepatitis, Influenza, Injections, Measles, Mumps, Polio, Rubella, Tetanus, Tuberculosis, Viruses, Whooping Cough

Immunity means that the body is immune to (protected against) certain diseases, for example infections caused by viruses. Natural immunity happens when the body catches an infection and suffers from it. The body's self-defence immune system learns to recognize and kill the viruses. If the same types of viruses enter the body later, the immune system destroys them before they cause illness.

Vaccines

Immunity can be given by putting vaccines into the body. Vaccines contain altered versions of the viruses or the harmful substances – toxins (poisons) – they make. These altered versions do not cause disease. But the body's immune system learns to destroy them in the same way as it does with natural immunity. Putting vaccines into the body is called vaccination – becoming resistant is immunization.

Injections or jabs

Most vaccines are injected, although some, such as polio, can be swallowed. Some vaccines cause mild discomfort or slight fever, but serious side-effects are very rare. A doctor can advise on all these issues.

Which diseases?

Immunization is usually carried out against polio (poliomyelitis), diphtheria, whooping cough (pertussis), tetanus, measles, mumps, rubella (German measles), perhaps tuberculosis (TB) using the BCG vaccine, and for older people, influenza (flu). Some of these are given in one combined vaccination, such as MMR (measles+mumps+rubella).

People at risk of catching infections because of their job, lifestyle or where they travel may receive extra vaccines such as hepatitis, typhoid and yellow fever.

In rare cases when a person already has a certain illness or condition, or a family history of a certain condition, a particular immunization may be not advised. This is called a contraindication.

DID YOU KNOW?

Immunization is one of greatest of all medical advances, and saves millions of lives every year. Researchers are trying to find new vaccines against infections such as HIV/AIDS and malaria.

INFECTIONS
See also Bacteria, Germs and Infection, Viruses

An infection occurs when microscopic germs – tiny living things such as bacteria, viruses or protists – enter the body and multiply to cause illness.

INFLUENZA (FLU)
See also Colds and the Common Cold, Germs and Infection, SARS, Viruses

The viral infection influenza is similar to a cold but more severe. Symptoms include headache, fever, sweats and chills, runny nose, coughing and aches and pains. The main treatment is to rest, have lots of drinks and take medicines such as paracetamol while the body conquers the virus.

Old, young and already sick people are at greater risk and should be seen by a doctor. Older people and other at-risk groups can be immunized every year before the winter.

INJECTIONS
See also AIDS and HIV, Drugs, Hepatitis, Immunity andImmunizations

An injection puts a substance through the skin into the body, using a hypodermic needle and a syringe or container. Injected substances include vaccines, drugs and extra fluids. Using an unclean needle and syringe previously used by another person can spread infections such as hepatitis and HIV/AIDS.

INTESTINES
See also Appendix, Rectum, Stomach and Digestion

The intestines are coiled into the lower body or abdomen, and make up the main length of the digestive tube. They are often called bowels, or along with the stomach, guts. The small intestine is 6 metres long and 3-4 cm wide. It takes in nutrients from digested food. The large intestine is 1.5 metres long and 6-7 cm wide, and takes in water while forming the leftovers into lumpy brown faeces (poo).

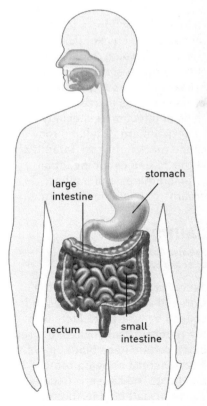

The intestines take up about half of the space in the abdomen.

ITCHING AND SCRATCHING

*See also Dermatitis, Eczema,
Germs and Infections, Skin and Touch*

Itchy feelings on the skin have many causes – a speck of dust, a hair poking in, an insect or similar small creature moving, biting or stinging, a nettle or similar plant sting, a wound repairing itself, a small area of infection such as a boil, or a harmful chemical in contact with the skin. Itching is also part of conditions such as eczema (dermatitis) and jaundice, and occurs with the spots and rashes of infections such as measles and chickenpox.

A quick scratch usually helps. But too much scratching may break the skin so that it weeps or bleeds. This increases the risks of infection (especially if fingernails are dirty) and may cause marks or scars later. It's better to use calamine lotion, antihistamines and similar creams to ease the problem.

JAUNDICE

*See also Gall Bladder, Hepatitis,
Liver and Bile*

Jaundice is a yellowing of the skin and whites of the eyes. It is caused by waste products from the natural breakdown of old red blood cells. These build up in the blood instead of being removed in bile fluid. The cause is usually a liver or gall bladder problem such as hepatitis or gallstones.

JOINTS

*See also Arthritis, Bones and Skeleton,
Cartilage, Dislocations, Hip, Knee,
Ligaments, Rheumatism, Sprains,
Tendons*

A joint is the point at which two bones meet. The body has more than 200 joints. Some are fixed or immovable, such as the rigid joints which form wiggly lines between the separate bones of the skull. Others are flexible or moveable so that you can bend, twist and straighten your body.

Types of joint

• Ball-and-socket joints are in the shoulder and hip. They allow up-and-down, side-to-side and twisting movements.

• Hinge joints are in the smaller knuckles and knee. These joints can only move backwards and forwards.

• Gliding joints are in the wrist or ankle. They allow limited sliding movements.

• Saddle joints are in the thumb and big knuckles. The bones in these joints butt together and allow sliding and tilting movements.

• Tilting joints allow limited movement between the separate bones (vertebrae) of the backbone.

Joint stiffness

Joints which are not exercised regularly will slowly become less flexible as their ligaments stiffen. The muscles around the joints also weaken. This eventually leads to aches and pains, which may mean that the joints are used even less. This is an unhealthy cycle.

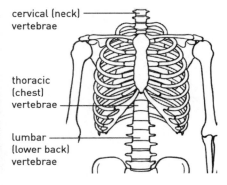

cervical (neck) vertebrae

thoracic (chest) vertebrae

lumbar (lower back) vertebrae

The vertebral bones of the back are separated by cartilage pads or discs.

Joint structure

In a typical joint, the bone ends are covered with smooth, shiny cartilage which reduces rubbing and wear on the bone. The joint is surrounded by a bag-like synovial capsule containing thick, slippery synovial fluid. This works like lubricating oil to keep the bones moving smoothly. Stretchy, strap-like ligaments cover the capsule and link the bones to prevent them moving too far, which might cause dislocation.

A sprain happens when ligaments and other parts of the joint are wrenched, which causes pain and swelling.

Joint replacement

Artificial joints (called prostheses) can replace joints that become very stiff and painful, or have been seriously injured. Joints which are often replaced include the hip and knee. These bear the body's weight and if they become arthritic they limit how far and fast someone can move. They may cause constant pain that can even affect sleep. Less common replacements are the ankle, foot, shoulder, elbow and finger joints (knuckles).

Most artificial joints are made of a combination of hard, smooth metal and tough, long-lasting plastic composites, that allow the same range of movements as the original joint. Most older people can expect a replacement joint to last at least ten years. Younger patients may need further replacements, especially while their bodies are growing.

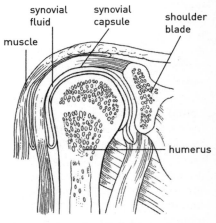

synovial fluid

synovial capsule

shoulder blade

muscle

humerus

The shoulder is the body's most flexible ball-and-socket joint.

KIDNEYS
See page 93

KNEE
*See also Arthritis, Bones and Skeleton,
Cartilage, Dislocations, Ligaments,
Muscles, Sprains, Tendons*

The knee is the joint where the
femur (thigh bone) meets the
tibia (shin bone). It is the biggest
single joint in the body.

The knee-cap or patella is
a small, flat triangular bone.
It is set into the main tendon
which runs from the thigh muscle
over the front of the knee to the
shin bone. It is not connected to
any other bone and is held in
place by muscles and ligaments.

Cartilage covers the lower
end of the femur and upper end
of the tibia to cushion the joint.
There are also two extra curved
pieces of cartilage called menisci
between the bones. The menisci
help the knee to lock when you
are standing upright.

Problems
Most knee problems are caused
by twisting to change direction
when running fast, for example
when playing sports such as
football and tennis.

Cartilage problems usually
involve the menisci, which can be
folded, worn, crushed or pop out
of position, and may need to be
removed in an operation.
Without the floating menisci, the
knee can still work fairly well, but
it is usually no longer able to cope
with great stress.

Ligament problems usually
involve the medial ligament on the
inner side of the knee (next to the
other knee), the lateral ligament
on the outside, or the two cruciate
ligaments which form a cross
or X shape inside the joint.

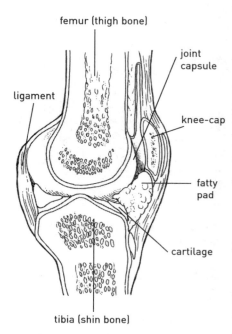

femur (thigh bone)

joint
capsule

ligament

knee-cap

fatty
pad

cartilage

tibia (shin bone)

**This cutaway of the knee joint
is seen from the side.**

Knee jerk
Tapping just below the knee-cap
(when sitting with the knee of one
leg over the knee of the other leg)
makes the lower leg flick or jerk
forward in a reflex reaction. This
is a common medical test for
nerve or muscle problems.

KIDNEYS

See also Bladder, Dialysis, Urine

The two kidneys are on either side of the backbone in the upper abdomen, just above waist height. Each is about half the size of a clenched fist. The kidneys filter blood passing through them and remove waste substances and unwanted water. These form urine (wee) which trickles down a tube called the ureter that connects each kidney to the bladder.

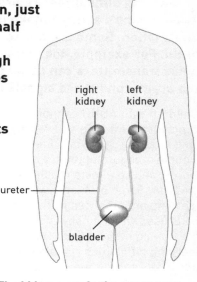

The kidneys are in the upper rear of the abdomen.

Inside a kidney

The outer layer of each kidney is the renal cortex. This contains more than a million tiny filters called nephrons, where wastes, minerals, salts and water are removed from blood. The middle layer, the renal medulla, has microscopic tubes from the filters where some of the minerals, salts and water pass back into the blood. The leftover urine flows into the space in the middle of the kidney, called the renal pelvis. This narrows to form the ureter which passes down to the bladder.

Problems and treatments

Sometimes hard lumps called kidney stones form in the renal pelvis. These can be dissolved with drugs or shattered into tiny pieces by ultrasound. One of the most common kidney problems is nephritis, an inflammation of the kidney's filtering units. Symptoms include oedema (a build-up of body fluid especially around joints), pain in the back or sides, blood in the urine and excess urine. Renal or kidney failure happens when the kidneys no longer do their job and wastes build up in the blood. It can be treated by dialysis or a transplant.

DID YOU KNOW?

The kidneys receive more blood per minute for their size than any other body part. In one day all the body's blood passes through the kidneys more than 300 times.

LEARNING DIFFICULTIES (specific)

See also ADHD, Brain and Thinking, Dyslexia, Ears and Hearing, Eyes and Seeing

Learning difficulties are problems that can affect someone's ability to take in, understand and remember information. Some are due to the chemical workings of the brain. For example, too many or too few of substances called neurotransmitters can upset the flow of nerve signals around the brain – and these signals are thoughts and information.

Children with ADHD cannot concentrate for long and rapidly lose interest. Dyslexia brings trouble recognizing letters and words, and so affects reading and spelling. Some problems with learning are inherited or they may be caused when a baby is developing in the womb. But learning difficulties can also occur for other different reasons.

Some causes of learning difficulties

• An infection such as encephalitis (swelling and inflammation of the brain, often due to infection by germs), which may cause few symptoms other than confused thinking.

• Difficulty with hearing, perhaps as a result of an ear infection, or difficulty in seeing clearly, due to a need for spectacles.

• Family or social problems such as bullying or a difficult home life.

• Eating foods which contain too many chemicals, such as additives and preservatives.

Recognition and treatment

A learning difficulty may have nothing to do with a child's general intelligence; it just means that part of the learning process does not work well.

At first a problem may show itself in behaviour such as crying, frustration or temper tantrums, especially in very young children. Older children can develop tricks or ways of disguising the problem (sometimes without realizing) which can make it difficult to assess when they have learning difficulties.

It's vital to identify the cause of a difficulty, with help from the family, teachers, doctors, and perhaps educational experts and others. As soon as this is done, then teaching methods, activities, and perhaps medical treatment such as drugs, can start to reduce the effects of any problem.

It's important for children to catch up with learning as quickly as possible. Support and understanding are also vital from family and friends – especially classmates.

LEUKAEMIAS

See also AIDS and HIV, Blood, Cancers, Cells, Tissues and Organs, Immunity, Lymph Fluid and Glands

Leukaemias are types of cancers that develop when white blood cells multiply out of control. White cells are part of the body's immune (self-defence) system. They kill germs and other invaders, and clean the blood.

Leukaemia occurs when abnormal white blood cells multiply rapidly and collect in the bone marrow where they develop, crowding out other, normal blood cells. They clog up blood vessels and the lymph nodes or glands where they gather. Acute leukaemias come on quickly; chronic ones are slower-developing. The main signs are swollen glands and general ill health.

There are many forms of treatment, depending on the type of leukaemia. They include chemotherapy and other medical drugs, radiotherapy (X-rays) and bone marrow transplants.

LICE

See also Fleas, Skin and Touch

The louse is a tiny insect which lives on the skin or among hairs. It has hook-shaped legs which cling strongly, and a needle-like mouth to pierce skin and suck blood, leaving itchy red marks. Head lice affect scalp hair. Body lice live mainly in clothes and usually go on to the skin only to feed. Crab or pubic lice affect the pubic or genital region (between the legs). Lice spread fast where people are close together, for example head lice in schools or crab lice during sex.

Treatments

Lotions and shampoos get rid of lice and their tiny white eggs or nits, which stick to hairs like grains of salt. Clothes infested with body lice or nits are best thrown away. In schools it's important that everyone is treated when there is an outbreak.

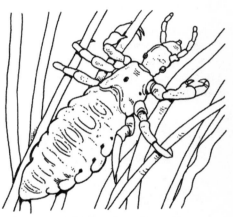

Treatment for head lice includes regular combing with a nit comb, but this only works if everyone in the family and class does it.

WHAT PEOPLE SAY

Lice only like dirty hair.
Not necessarily. Even people with clean, freshly-washed hair can quickly catch head lice.

LIGAMENTS

See also Bones and Skeleton, Dislocations, Joints, Knee, Sprains, Tendons

Ligaments are strong, slightly stretchy straps that join the ends of bones in a joint. They stop the bones from moving too far and dislocating the joint. A sprained joint usually includes wrenched ligaments.

LIVER AND BILE

See also Food and Eating, Gall Bladder, Hepatitis, Jaundice, Stomach and Digestion, Vitamins

The liver is the biggest part in the body, and has more tasks than any other part – more than 500. It is brown and wedge-shaped, and is in the upper right abdomen.

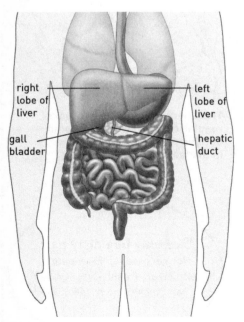

right lobe of liver

left lobe of liver

gall bladder

hepatic duct

The bulk of the liver is in the upper left abdomen.

What the liver does

• Receives digested nutrients direct from the intestines.

• Breaks down part-digested nutrients into smaller ones.

• Stores or releases these nutrients when needed.

• Breaks down or detoxifies harmful substances, such as alcohol, into harmless ones.

• Makes certain vitamins, and stores other vitamins and minerals.

• Changes blood glucose (sugar) into starch and stores this when blood glucose is high, or does the reverse when blood glucose is low.

• Breaks down and recycles old red blood cells.

Bile

The liver makes a thick, bitter, greenish-brown fluid called bile from the breakdown of red blood cells and other substances. Bile is stored in the liver and in a small bag underneath called the gall bladder. After a meal, bile flows along the bile ducts into the small intestine where it helps digestion. Bile helps to digest fatty foods by breaking up (or emulsifying) blobs and drops of fat and oil.

Liver problems

Infection or inflammation of the liver is called hepatitis, and one of its main symptoms is jaundice. Cirrhosis is damage and scarring of the liver, and is usually caused by drinking too much alcohol.

LUNGS AND BREATHING

See also Bronchitis, Oxygen, Pneumonia, Smoking, Tobacco

The gas oxygen in the air is needed by almost every living thing – including humans. We take in oxygen by breathing air through the nose and mouth. The air passes down the windpipe (trachea) which branches into two wide tubes called bronchi, one for each lung. The bronchi branch many times, becoming narrower, until they form bronchioles, which are thinner than hairs.

At the end of each bronchiole is a group of tiny bubbles called alveoli, which are filled with air. There are 300 million alveoli in each lung, giving a surface area as big as a tennis court to take in the amount of oxygen the body needs. The alveoli are surrounded by microscopic blood vessels called capillaries. Oxygen in the air seeps out of the alveoli into the blood in the capillaries to be carried around the body. At the same time waste carbon dioxide seeps the other way, from blood to air, and is breathed out.

Breathing rate

At rest most people breathe about 15 times per minute, taking in and blowing out half a litre of air each time. After activity the rate can go up to around 50 breaths per minute with three litres of air per breath. The main breathing muscles are the dome-shaped diaphragm below the lungs, and the long, narrow intercostals between the ribs. When these muscles contract, the lungs enlarge to suck in air. When they relax, the stretched, elastic lungs spring back to their smaller size.

The tops of the lungs extend above the level of the collar bones. The right lung is shown in cutaway.

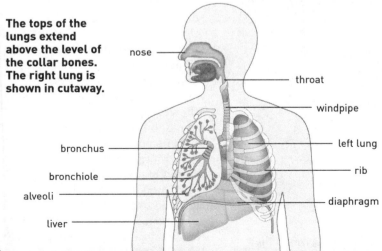

- nose
- throat
- windpipe
- bronchus
- bronchiole
- alveoli
- liver
- left lung
- rib
- diaphragm

LYMPH FLUID AND NODES (GLANDS)

See also Blood, Glands, Immunity and Immunizations, Spleen, Thymus Gland

Pale, milky lymph fluid collects around and between body tissues and body parts. It slowly channels into lymph vessel tubes which take it to the chest, where two main lymph ducts empty the fluid into the main veins. Lymph fluid carries nutrients around the body, collects wastes and contains microscopic white blood cells to fight disease. Some lymph vessels have blob-like widened parts called lymph nodes packed with white cells, especially those called lymphocytes.

thoracic duct

axillary (armpit) lymph nodes

spleen

intestinal lymph nodes

inguinal (groin) lymph nodes

lymph vessels

Lymph vessels collect lymph fluid from most areas of the body.

There are groups of lymph nodes (sometimes called glands) in the neck, armpits and groin.

ME (MYALGIC ENCEPHALOMYELITIS)

See also Brain and Thinking, Depression, Infections, Viruses

ME, also known as Chronic Fatigue Syndrome, is a rare and mysterious illness which may be triggered by a viral infection. Sufferers are tired, have muscle pains, cannot concentrate, have poor memory and depression. There is no specific treatment. Most sufferers recover over several months or maybe longer.

MEASLES

See also Immunity and Immunization, Rashes, Viruses

Measles is a very infectious viral illness. It spreads very fast and its side effects include an increased risk of catching other infections, for example conjunctivitis in the eyes, ear infections, and lung infections such as pneumonia. These can be serious. The sufferer has a fever, runny nose and sore eyes. Tiny white spots develop in the mouth, followed by itchy spots on the head and body, less commonly on arms and legs. The spots grow, merge and fade over a week. Lotions can help reduce the itching. Measles should be reported to a doctor. It is now rare in countries such as Britain where most children are immunized with the MMR vaccine.

MELANIN
See also Hair, Skin and Touch, Sunburn

Melanin is a dark brown or black pigment (coloured substance) in skin and hair. It is made by melanocyte cells at the base of the skin's outer layer, the epidermis. The amount of melanin the cells make is controlled by genes inherited from your parents.

The more melanin you have, the darker your skin. When you are exposed to sunlight, your skin produces more melanin, which darkens your skin. However, this happens slowly, and if pale skin is suddenly exposed to the sun, it cannot prevent the skin becoming red and inflamed, or sunburnt.

Taking care in the sun
Exposure to the sun's rays should be gradual and limited. Use clothes, hats and sunscreen as protection, and take care to stay in the shade during the hottest part of the day from noon to 3pm. Too much exposure to the sun can result in a form of skin cancer linked to melanin production called malignant melanoma.

MEMORY
See also Brain and Thinking

The brain stores all kinds of information as memories – not only facts, names and words, but sights, sounds, smells and emotions. Memories are probably routes or pathways among the billions of interconnected nerve cells (neurons) in the brain.

There is no single memory centre – memories seem to be spread out among various brain parts, including the upper surface or cortex and the hippocampus in the middle. The memory system can improve with use and training. Various memory tricks can help learning, such as making pictures or phrases from information.

Short-term memory is the brain's notebook for recalling information that probably will not be needed again, such as a phone number used only occasionally.

More important information is transferred to long-term memory. Recalling a memory regularly can help to refresh and prolong it, perhaps by reinforcing its pathways between neurons.

MENINGITIS
See also Brain and Thinking, Headaches, Immunity and Immunization, Germs and Infections, Rashes, Viruses

Meningitis is the swelling or inflammation of the meninges, the three thin layers covering the brain and spinal cord. It is usually the result of a viral or bacterial infection. Meningitis can be very serious, especially for young children, so it needs urgent medical attention.

Signs include fever, headache, vomiting, drowsiness, stiff neck, perhaps a skin rash, and inability to tolerate bright light. Bacterial meningitis may occur in small epidemics. People at risk can be vaccinated against it.

MENSTRUAL CYCLE
See also Periods and Menstrual Cycle

The menstrual cycle is the process of preparing and releasing an egg cell, and preparing the lining of the womb (uterus) to nourish it, if it is joined by a sperm cell to start the growth of a baby.

METABOLISM
See also Hormones, Thyroid Gland

The body is, in effect, a huge mass of chemical changes and reactions. Millions of substances are built up, altered and broken down every second inside billions of microscopic cells. All these reactions and changes together are known as metabolism.
An example is the breakdown of blood sugar, glucose, to release its energy for powering muscles. The rate of metabolism is affected by certain hormones, including thyroxine from the thyroid gland.

MIGRAINE
See also Headaches, Meningitis

Migraines are severe, intense headaches that can last for several hours. The feeling is often worse on one side of the head. Other symptoms accompany the headache, such as feeling sick, vomiting, dizziness, fear of bright lights, and sight problems such as mistiness, flashes or zigzags. Some people have a warning sign or aura such as a strange taste in the mouth or pins-and-needles.

Cause and treatment
The causes of migraine are unclear, although the problem can be passed down in families. At the onset of a migraine the blood vessels in the brain become narrower, then wider, which may cause the pain. Some sufferers find the headache is set off or triggered by a substance or event – ranging from cheese or chocolate to a sudden fright. Lying in a quiet, darkened room can help to ease the pain, as can various medical drugs.

MINERALS
See also Anaemia, Diets and Dieting, Food and Eating, Vitamins

The body needs around 50 minerals for health. They are mostly single chemical substances such as fluorine for strong teeth, zinc for healthy skin and iodine for thyroid gland hormones. A healthy balanced diet usually contains enough minerals of all kinds.

Foods containing zinc

Foods containing iodine

Foods containing fluorine

Foods containing iron

Some people may need extra minerals as supplements or pills, such as iron tablets for some forms of anaemia.

MOLES
See also Freckles, Growths, Melanin, Skin and Touch, Spots and Skin Marks

Moles are small dark areas on the skin, which may be slightly raised. Their dark colour is caused by clumps of melanin cells in the skin. Moles usually develop during childhood, and almost everyone has a few of them. A prominent mole that causes distress can be removed by a small operation.

A mole that changes for no obvious reason – grows darker, swells, becomes sore or starts to bleed – should be shown to a doctor in case it is some form of more serious skin growth.

MUMPS
See also Immunity and Immunization, Infections, Saliva, Testes

Mumps is a viral infection that tends to occur in childhood and affects the six salivary glands in the face which make saliva (spit). The glands swell and become very tender, especially the parotid salivary gland just below and in front of each ear. Some boys also suffer from swollen and tender testes (testicles). The main treatment is bed rest and pain-killers such as ibuprofen. Mumps should be reported to a doctor. It is rare in countries such as Britain where children are immunized with the MMR vaccine.

MUSCLES

See also Bones and Skeleton, Brain and Thinking, Cramps, Exercise and Fitness, Tendons

Muscles are tough, flexible parts in the body that adjust their length by shortening or contracting, to create the forces needed to make us move. The body has three kinds of muscle. Cardiac muscle (myocardium) forms the walls of the heart. This powerful muscle contracts to pump blood out of the heart every second of your life.

Visceral (involuntary or smooth) muscles form layers in the walls of the gullet, stomach, intestines, ureters, bladder and other inner parts. They work largely under automatic control, without us having to think about them.

Skeletal (voluntary or striped) muscles are attached to bones. The muscles pull on the bones to move the body. They work when we order them to contract by sending signals called motor impulses from the brain. There are about 640 skeletal muscles. The biggest is the gluteus maximus, which forms most of the buttock. It pulls the thigh bone back when we walk, run and jump.

Superficial muscles are those under the skin.

frontalis

platysma

deltoid

pectoralis

biceps

trapezius

rectus abdomin

external oblique

sartorius

rectus femoris

vastus medialis

gastrocnemius

tibialis anterior

Inside a muscle

A muscle contains bundles of hair-thin myofibres. Each of these is a bundle of microscopic myofibrils which contain long, rope-like molecules of the substances actin and myosin. When these substances slide past each other, the whole muscle shortens. A muscle has a nerve to control its contraction, and blood vessels to bring glucose (blood sugar) to power contraction. The blood vessels also take away wastes such as lactic acid which might otherwise cause cramps.

Muscle health

Muscles become bigger, more effective, and less likely to strain or tear with regular exercise and activity. Diseases of the muscles are rare. Muscular dystrophy, which is mainly inherited, is a disease in which the muscles are weak, difficult to control and waste away. But most muscle problems, such as paralysis (inability to move), are caused by the muscles' blood supply or the nerves controlling them.

WHAT PEOPLE SAY

He's got more muscles than me!

Everyone has the same number of muscles. Regular use and exercise does not make extra ones. But it does builds muscle bulk by making individual muscles larger and stronger.

NAILS
See also Hair, Skin and Touch

Fingernails and toenails are made of the tough substance keratin, which also forms hairs and the outer layer of skin. A nail grows from its root, hidden under the cuticle – the edge of skin that lies over the nail. The nail slides slowly along the nail bed (the flat surface under the nail) towards the tip of the finger or toe. The pale crescent-shaped part of the nail is called the lunula.

Most people's nails grow about half a millimetre each week. They are best washed daily and cut straight across with a nail trimmer or nail scissors.

Nail problems

Odd coloured nails may be due to an illness, poor food or perhaps a fungal nail infection which can be treated with medicinal cream. Injury can cause the nail bed to bruise and the nail to turn black. This dark area gradually grows out and can be trimmed away.

NECK
See also Accidents and Emergencies, Bones and Skeleton, Nerves

Anyone who suffers neck injury, especially whiplash in a car accident, may have damaged the spinal cord and should move the neck as little as possible. If there is loss of feeling, inability to move or pins and needles, the person should not be moved until emergency medical help arrives.

NERVES

See also Brain and Thinking, Pins and Needles, Spina Bifida

Nerves are string-like parts that connect the brain to all body parts. They carry nerve signals, which are tiny pulses of electricity, each one-tenth of a volt for one-thousandth of a second. Thousands of signals flash along the nerve network every second, at speeds of 1 to 100 metres per second. Sensory nerve signals pass from the eyes, ears, nose, tongue and skin to the brain. Motor nerve signals pass from the brain to control the muscles and glands.

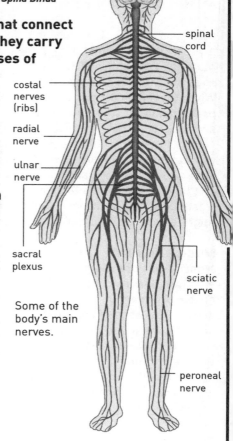

Some of the body's main nerves.

A typical nerve has a strong outer covering wrapped around bundles of nerve fibres, each too thin to see. These fibres are long, drawn-out parts of nerve cells (neurones). Around each fibre is a layer of fatty substance called myelin sheath, which is like the plastic insulation around an electrical wire.

Nerve problems

Motor neurone disease, MND, is a condition in which the motor nerves controlling muscles decay and die, so the muscles waste away. Multiple sclerosis, MS, occurs as a result of damage to the myelin around nerve fibres. It causes problems such as trembling and stiffness or paralysis.

Neuritis is the swelling and inflammation of nerves, usually due to infection or injury.

It causes pins and needles, lack of sensations and problems in controlling muscles.

Damage

Nerve cells are very specialized, so damage to them takes a long time to heal – if it ever does. Someone who has an accident such as a car crash or fall should not be moved until expert help arrives, as this may worsen any nerve damage.

NOSE AND SMELL

See also Cartilage, Lungs and Breathing, Nosebleeds, Senses, Sinuses

Most of the air we breathe in and out goes through the nose. Just inside the nostrils, tiny hairs filter out floating bits of dust and particles. The nose's inner lining of sticky mucus (snot) traps dust and germs and moistens the air, while the plentiful blood vessels in its lining warm the air before it goes into the lungs.

Rhinitis is the swelling and inflammation of the nose lining as a result of a cold or an allergy such as hay fever.

The nose is made of curved plates of flexible cartilage (gristle). The nostrils lead into matchbox-sized air spaces or nasal chambers, separated by a central wall of cartilage called the septum. At the rear the chambers join and lead down, around the back of the palate (roof of the mouth) and mouth, to the throat. Openings from the nasal chambers lead to dead-end air spaces within the bones of the face and skull, called sinuses.

Smell

In the upper part of each nasal chamber is a hairy-looking patch about the size of a thumbnail. This patch, called the olfactory epithelium, contains more than 10 million microscopic cells which detect smells or odours as tiny particles floating in air. Most people can tell apart up to 10,000 different scents and smells.

Sniffing makes air swirl around the top of the nasal chamber, nearer the olfactory epithelium, and so improves smell.

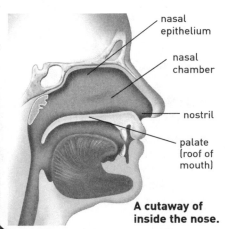

nasal epithelium

nasal chamber

nostril

palate (roof of mouth)

A cutaway of inside the nose.

When I have a cold, food loses its taste.

What we think of as taste is smell and taste combined. Odours waft from chewed food around the back of the mouth and up into the nose. A cold blocks the nose with mucus so smells are much reduced, although taste works normally.

NOSEBLEEDS
See also Bleeding, Nose and Smell

The lining inside the nose is very thin and contains plentiful blood vessels. An injury to the nose or blowing it too hard may break the lining and cause a nosebleed. Rarely a nosebleed is a side-effect of medical drugs. Some people have nosebleeds for no apparent reason.

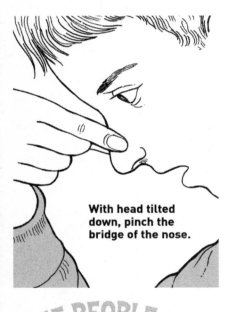

With head tilted down, pinch the bridge of the nose.

WHAT PEOPLE SAY

Nosebleeds are nature's way of lowering high blood pressure.
There is hardly ever a connection between high blood pressure and frequent nosebleeds.

Treatment
Lean forward and pinch the bridge of the nose for 5-10 minutes. If the bleeding continues, repeat the process. Spit out any blood in your mouth as swallowing it may make you feel sick. Afterwards, try not to blow your nose for a few hours. Nosebleeds which last longer than 30 minutes need medical help.

NURSES
See also Doctors, Health Workers, Hospitals

Nurses are trained to take care of ill people and carry out procedures such as giving injections, measuring blood pressure and stitching wounds.

General practice (GP) nurses undertake a wide range of tasks, while nurses in hospitals usually specialize in a group of health problems, such as mental health, or a group of patients, such as babies. Increasingly, nurses with medical qualifications undertake jobs which traditionally have been done by doctors, for example, prescribing drugs.

In Britain the main nursing qualification is RN, which stands for Registered Nurse.

NUTRITION
See also Diets and Dieting, Food and Eating

Nutrition is the process of eating and digesting food. It is also the study of the body's food needs and how different types of nutrients affect health.

OBESITY

See also Anorexia and Bulimia, Calories, Diets and Dieting, Energy,
Exercise and Fitness, Food and Eating, Stomach and Digestion, Weight

Obese people are overweight, usually because they have too much body fat. Most ways of defining obesity use the BMI – Body Mass Index. This is weight in kilograms divided by height in metres multiplied by itself: $W \div (H \times H)$. A BMI of less than 25 is not obese; one of over 40 is very obese.

The basic cause of obesity is eating too much. Extra food supplies more energy than the body needs, so the energy is changed to fat and stored. This can happen for several reasons.

- Taking too little exercise.

- Sitting still for long periods, for example in front of the TV or computer.

- Eating for something to do, to relieve stress or as comfort.

- Over-eating as a habit from younger times, especially early childhood.

- Eating too much of the wrong type of foods, such as energy-rich sugars, carbohydrates and fats.

The risks of obesity

A full list of the risks of obesity would fill many pages. They include heart and blood vessel problems, some forms of diabetes, joint strains, muscle sprains, shortness of breath, lung and breathing troubles, gall bladder disease, some cancers, and many other health-related problems.

Treating obesity

The basic treatment for obesity is simple: eat less.

- Reduce food intake by eating smaller portions.

- Eat less food that is rich in fats, sugars and starches.

- Eat more foods which contain plentiful fibre (especially fresh vegetables). These give bulk which helps to satisfy the appetite and keeps the digestive passageway healthy.

- Take more exercise. This can be swimming, cycling, gym, ballet, football or walking, to burn off stored energy and benefit the whole body.

- Use self control in situations where too much food is available, for example, meal binges, blow-outs with friends, or when you feel like eating a quick bar of chocolate, or packet of biscuits. Say no when you've eaten enough. Even if you still feel peckish get into the habit of refusing more food, rather than the habit of accepting it. Don't eat for the sake of eating.

OPERATIONS

See also Anaesthetics, Doctors, Hospitals, Nurses, Physiotherapy

An operation is something done to the body usually by hands, especially surgery using tools such as scalpels (very sharp blades) and other equipment. Operations range from putting a dislocated joint back in position, to complicated procedures lasting hours, involving teams of specialist surgeons, anaesthetists, nurses and support staff.

Anaesthetic (which means without feeling) dulls or removes sensations or feelings, mainly touch and pain. A local anaesthetic affects just part of the body, and is usually given by injection. Under a local anaesthetic people stay aware or conscious. A general anaesthetic affects the whole body and usually puts the person 'to sleep' for a time. It is generally given by injection, passed into the bloodstream as a drip, or as a breathed-in gas.

Minor and major

Most minor operations can be done under local anaesthetic, for example fillings at the dentist. People having this sort of operation do not stay in hospital overnight. Some family doctors (GPs or general practitioners) carry out minor operations at health centres or clinics, often called surgeries. Or an operation may be done at a small local hospital. A major operation usually involves a general anaesthetic and the patient stays in hospital for a night or longer.

Pre- and post-op

Pre-op (meaning before the operation) is a general term for preparing someone for surgery. It usually involves a final check on the problem and perhaps medical drugs to relax the muscles.

Post-op refers to after the operation, when a patient may need special care such as a heart monitor or a drip which puts fluids into a vein. Today patients are encouraged to move around as soon as possible after an operation, with the help of physiotherapy and other treatments. This helps the body to heal faster – and also frees hospital beds for waiting patients.

DID YOU KNOW?

An operating theatre is so named because many years ago people paid to come and watch a surgeon's skills and performance, as they would an actor in a real theatre.

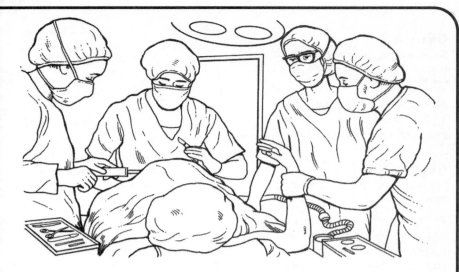

Surgeons and nurses work as a team during operations.

Operation words

xxxxx-ectomy Taking out or removing a body part, as in appendectomy, removing the appendix.

Arthroscopy Endoscopy into a joint (see below).

Biopsy Removing a small part or sample – sometimes as tiny as a pin-head – to study it in a medical laboratory, for example, to check it is not cancerous.

Bronchoscopy Endoscopy down the throat and windpipe into the main airways of the lungs (see below).

Endoscopy Putting a viewing device into the body, such as a bendy telescope, to look inside. This can be done through a natural body opening such as the mouth, or through a small cut or incision.

Gastroscopy Endoscopy into the stomach.

Keyhole surgery An operation done through a very small cut or incision, rather than cutting open a whole area.

Laparoscopy Endoscopy into the abdomen or tummy.

Laser surgery Using laser beams of high-energy light to cut, shape and join body parts, especially inside the eye.

Proctoscopy Endoscopy into the end of the digestive system, the rectum or anus.

Prosthesis An artificial or man-made body part, such as an artificial hip joint, implanted into the body.

Theatre The specially-equipped, extremely clean room where operations take place.

ORGANS

See also Cells, Tissue and Organs, Brain and Thinking, Heart and Pulse and other major body parts

An organ is a main part of the body: the brain, heart, lungs, liver and kidneys are all organs.

OVARIES

See also Periods and Menstrual Cycle, Sexual Organs

The two ovaries in the lower abdomen (tummy) of the female body are organs which make egg cells that can grow into new babies.

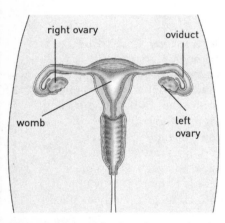

The ovaries are the female sex glands.

OXYGEN

See also Choking, Energy, Lungs and Breathing, Metabolism

Nearly all living things, including plants, microbes, animals and humans, need a regular supply of oxygen to survive. Oxygen is a gas with no colour, taste or smell. It forms one-fifth of the invisible air around us. We breathe it into our lungs and our blood carries it around the body. Oxygen helps to break apart the body's main energy source, blood sugar (glucose), inside its microscopic cells. As sugar is split, it releases its energy in chemical form. Cells use this energy for the thousands of life processes and chemical changes taking place inside them every second, which are together known as the body's metabolism.

Oxygen for life

The body cannot store oxygen or survive for more than a few minutes without oxygen, or it will be damaged, especially the heart and brain. If the lungs are starved of oxygen, for example through choking, strangulation or drowning, this will harm or even kill someone through suffocation.

PAEDIATRICIAN

See also Babies and Infants, Doctors, Hospitals, Nurses

A paediatrician is a medical doctor who specializes in caring for babies and children. This includes checking their condition just before, during and straight after birth, and also following their growth and development, and identifying and treating illnesses.

Some health problems affect only children. Other illnesses may affect babies or children very differently from an adult, so they need different types of care. A paediatric nurse is a nurse who specializes in a similar way.

PANCREAS

See also Diabetes, Enzymes, Glands, Hormones, Stomach and Digestion

The pancreas is part of both the digestive and hormonal systems. It is a long, wedge-shaped organ in the upper rear left of the abdomen (tummy), below and behind the stomach.

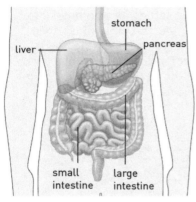

stomach

pancreas

liver

small intestine

large intestine

The pancreas is mostly behind the stomach, with its blunt end (head) and tubes into the intestine facing right.

Roles of the pancreas

• **The pancreas makes powerful digestive juices containing chemicals called enzymes. Every day about one litre of pancreatic juices passes along the pancreatic duct (tube) into the small intestine, to break down food.**

• **The pancreas also makes the hormones insulin and glucagon. These pass into the blood and affect the way the body uses blood sugar, glucose, as its main energy source. Problems with making or using insulin cause diabetes.**

PARACETAMOL

See also Aspirin, Drugs

Paracetamol is one of the best known pain-killers or analgesic (pain-reducing) medical drugs. For children, it is usually safer than aspirin, but take the advice of a pharmacist or doctor, and read the instructions that come with it, as for any medical drug. You can find paracetamol in many over-the-counter pain-relief pills, powders and other preparations.

An overdose of paracetamol causes liver damage and is very dangerous, but this may not be obvious until several days after taking the drug. Anyone suspected of taking a paracetamol overdose needs urgent hospital attention even if he or she seems fine.

PENIS

See also Bladder, Sex, Sexual Organs, Urine, Vagina

The penis is one of the male sexual or reproductive parts, and also part of the urinary (excretory) system. A tube, the ureter, runs along its length and opens at the end. The ureter carries urine outside the body from the bladder during urination (weeing or peeing). During sexual activity it also carries sperm-containing fluid called semen.

After puberty, the penis becomes larger and stiffer when sexually aroused. This is called erection and it allows the penis to deliver sperm into the vagina of a woman during sexual intercourse.

PERIODS AND MENSTRUAL CYCLE

See also Contraception, Hormones, Ovaries, Pregnancy, Puberty, Sex, Sexual Organs

The menstrual cycle is a series of changes in the female body that prepare for pregnancy and the growth of a baby. The cycle usually lasts about 28 days. It begins with a period or menstruation (sometimes called the curse).

For about four days the thickened lining of the womb (uterus) loses blood, which flows from the vagina. From then on the womb lining begins to thicken again and a tiny egg cell ripens in the ovary. The egg cell is released on or about day 14. If it joins (or is fertilized by) a male sperm cell, a tiny embryo starts to develop and settles (or implants) into the womb lining, which then does not bleed. If the egg is not fertilized it becomes part of the next period as the womb sheds its lining again.

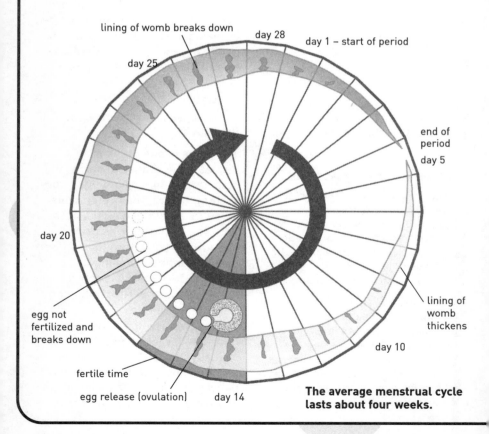

The average menstrual cycle lasts about four weeks.

Period problems

The pattern of periods is called the menstrual cycle. It is controlled by a delicate balance of several hormones – mainly oestrogen and progesterone. Menstrual cycles may vary with illness, great stress, severe emotions or for no obvious reason at all.

Rarely, period pains or cramps (called dysmenorrhoea) have an underlying cause such as infection or fibroids, so when they first happen, they should be reported to a doctor. If there is no serious cause, the doctor may advise ordinary pain-killing drugs or a type of contraceptive pill which changes the balance of hormones.

Some women occasionally miss a period. This is rarely serious, although it is usually an early sign of pregnancy.

Other period problems

Heavy periods, with lots of bleeding, are known as menorrhagia. They may also be very long – six days or more. As with painful periods, when they first occur, heavy periods should be reported to a doctor, who can check for any underlying problem. If they persist they can be treated with various medical drugs, or a type of contraceptive pill, or an operation called D&C (dilatation and curettage) where the part of the lining of the womb is scraped or removed.

Not having periods at all is called amenorrhoea. If this happens after puberty but before the usual time of the menopause (about 50-55 years of age) it may be due to severe weight loss or another problem and should receive medical attention. The weight loss of anorexia nervosa may cause periods to stop for a time.

Starting and finishing

Most girls start having periods during the time of puberty, between the ages of 11 and 13. The first full period at this time is called the menarche. But periods can begin anywhere between the ages of 10 and 20. When a woman is about 50, her periods usually become irregular for a time, with other signs such as hot flushes, then stop. This time is called the menopause.

WHAT PEOPLE SAY

Painful periods are a curse which women must endure.

There are various effective treatments for painful periods and similar problems. However some involve contraceptive pills, which may not be approved by certain religious, ethnic or cultural groups.

PERSONAL HYGIENE
See page 115

PERTUSSIS
See Whooping Cough page 155

PHOBIAS
See also Psychiatrist

A phobia is a great fear of an object or situation, for no sensible reason. British spiders are not huge, poisonous or dangerous, yet some people are not merely scared, but truly terrified of them. This fear is called arachnophobia. There are more than 200 named phobias, including fear of open places (agoraphobia) or enclosed spaces (claustrophobia). Most people cope with minor fears in daily life.

A severe phobia can be treated by types of behaviour therapy and perhaps medical drugs. For example, people can learn to confront a feared thing or place gradually in a series of small stages.

WHAT PEOPLE SAY

He's afraid of heights, which is vertigo

Vertigo is a feeling of giddiness, spinning or losing balance. Some people get this when they look down a long way. True fear of heights is called acrophobia.

PHYSIOTHERAPY
See also Cerebral Palsy, Cystic Fibrosis, Doctors, Exercise and Fitness, Health Workers, Joints, Muscles

Physiotherapy includes a wide range of physical therapies or treatments, including exercise, massage, movements, manipulation and heat. These mainly affect the body's muscles, joints and bones. Physiotherapists can treat various illnesses and conditions (such as cerebral palsy or cystic fibrosis). They also help injured people, or people who have suffered a long-term illness such as a stroke, back to normal activity.

PERSONAL HYGIENE

See also Bad Breath, Body Odour, Dentists, Feet, Hair, Nails, Skin and Touch, Sweat, Teeth

Most people avoid dirt, stains and unpleasant smells, especially on another person. This in-built or instinctive dislike is helpful as dirt and smells may be linked to germs and diseases. In countries such as Britain today most people have hot water, soap, shampoo and clean clothes, so there is rarely an excuse for poor personal hygiene – that is, not keeping clean.

Hygiene problems can sometimes be covered up or masked with sprays, scents and deodorants. But these don't solve the problem and do not reduce health risks such as skin spots and infections. It's not difficult to wash properly with soap and warm water every day, and to have an all-over bath or shower at least once every two or three days.

Thorough washing

Regular washing should include shampooing hair, scrubbing nails, washing between toes, under the arms, and under the foreskin of the penis for boys and men, as well as all the body's other nooks and crannies. Teeth should be cleaned regularly and mouthwashes used to avoid bad breath. Everyone needs to wash more often during hot and humid weather when our bodies lose water by sweating. Body odour (or BO) is often caused by dried, stale sweat.

Hygiene habits

Everyone should understand the health risks involved in poor hygiene and the effect it has on other people. Health workers, such as nurses at a local health centre or surgery, can give advice on this when needed.

Clean hands and clothing

Hands should always be washed after using the toilet, or after touching dirt, soil or chemicals. They should also be washed before mealtimes or when handling food. This helps to prevent problems such as food poisoning, as well as reducing the risk of spreading common germs such as cold viruses.

Dirt, germs and smells from dried body sweat can become worn into clothes, especially underwear and socks. These should be changed frequently – ideally every day.

PIERCING

See also Personal Hygiene, Skin and Touch

A small hole or gap can be pierced in almost any part of the body for almost any reason. Common sites are the ear lobes, navel (tummy button), nose, eyebrows, lips, and less obviously, sexual organs (genitals).

Piercing fashions come and go and often cause arguments, but there are a few basic guidelines.

Guidelines for piercing

• ALWAYS go to a qualified practitioner who uses sterile equipment with full hygiene precautions. Occasionally piercing can spread serious diseases such as hepatitis.

• Pay extra attention when washing or cleaning. If a piercing site is sore, check it with the local health centre or medical clinic, before infection or scarring gains a hold.

• You may not be allowed to wear studs or have other piercings in some schools, jobs or clubs.

• You should remove or tape over studs or rings before taking part in sports and activities, in case they injure you or others. This is a rule in many sports.

PIMPLES

See page 138

PINS AND NEEDLES

See also Nerves, Joints

Pins and needles (called paraesthesia) are buzzing or prickling feelings. They are usually caused by sitting or lying awkwardly, and squashing a nerve or its blood supply, or by a sudden knock that traps a nerve. The pins and needles usually fade when you move that part of the body. If they continue for no obvious reason, they should be reported to a doctor. In rare cases they may indicate an underlying disease.

PITUITARY

See also Brain and Thinking, Hormones

The pea-sized pituitary is a gland under the front of the brain. It produces more than ten hormones (body chemicals) which control major processes such as growth and sexual development, as well as hormones which control other hormonal glands.

pituitary

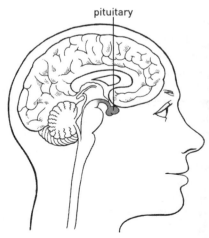

The pituitary is under the brain.

PNEUMONIA
See also Bacteria, Bronchitis, Infections, Lungs and Breathing, Oxygen, Viruses

Pneumonia is a serious infection of the lungs. It can be caused by bacterial or viral germs. It affects the tiny airways and microscopic air sacs (alveoli) in the lungs, while bronchitis affects mainly the larger airways.

Pneumonia often develops as a complication of another illness and causes coughing, wheezing, shortness of breath, fever and chest pains. Lobar pneumonia affects mainly one main section or segment (lobe) of one lung. Double-pneumonia affects both lungs.

Treatment
The main treatment for pneumonia is rest, perhaps with pain-relieving medicines and antibiotic drugs for bacterial infection. Sometimes pneumonia sufferers are taken to hospital and given oxygen-rich air to help their lungs take in enough oxygen.

WHAT PEOPLE SAY

I had a touch of pneumonia yesterday, but I'm all right now
Very unlikely. Real pneumonia is a serious, sometimes life-threatening disease.

When someone is already ill, pneumonia may be very serious, even fatal. Even otherwise healthy people can take weeks to recover.

PREGNANCY
See pages 118–119

PROTEINS
See also Diets and Dieting, Food and Eating

Proteins are substances in food that supply building materials for the body to grow, maintain and repair itself. They provide structural parts which are like tiny building blocks. There are proteins in meat, poultry, fish, dairy products, nuts and vegetables such as beans and peas.

High-protein foods are especially important for babies and young children because their bodies are growing fast. They are also important for some sports people, especially those involved in power sports such as sprinting and weight lifting.

PSYCHIATRIST
See also Brain and Thinking, Depression, Phobias

A psychiatrist is a qualified doctor who specializes in mental (mind-based) problems which affect how people behave, think, learn and react. In simple terms, a psychologist studies the normal mind and a psychiatrist treats the troubled or disturbed mind.

PREGNANCY

See also Abortion, Babies and Infants, Birth, Contraception, Genes and Inheritance, Periods and Menstrual Cycle, Ovaries, Puberty, Scans, Sex, Sexual Organs

During pregnancy a baby grows inside its mother's womb (uterus). Pregnancy lasts about nine months as the baby develops from a pinhead-sized egg into a fully-formed human being weighing about 3-3.5 kg.

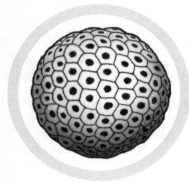

One week old – a hollow ball of cells called the blastocyst.

Conception

Pregnancy begins when a ripe egg cell from one of the mother's ovaries joins with a sperm cell from the father usually in the oviduct or fallopian tube (the tube between an ovary and the womb). This usually happens after sex (sexual intercourse). Assisted reproduction (also known as IVF – in-vitro fertilization or test-tube baby) mixes sperm and eggs in a dish. The joining of egg and sperm is called fertilization. It is sometimes called conception, but this term is also used when the fertilized egg settles or implants into the thickened, blood-rich lining of the womb, about a week later.

Embryo

For the first eight weeks, the tiny developing baby is called an embryo. It starts as a single cell, and divides many times into dozens, hundreds and thousands of cells. These move about to form body parts such as the brain, heart and stomach. At first the embryo is ball- and then disc-shaped, then it looks like a bent tadpole the length of this letter 'l'. As its face, arms and legs form, it starts to look like a tiny human and is about the size of a grape.

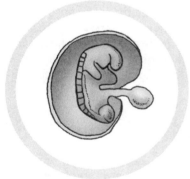

Four weeks old – brain, limb buds, tail.

Foetus

From eight weeks to birth, the developing baby is called a foetus (or fetus). It grows rapidly, and

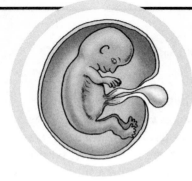

Eight weeks old – end of embryo stage.

details such as fingernails, toenails and eyelashes form. The fetus looks long and thin at first. But towards birth it puts on body fat and looks more like a chubby baby. It also grows a thin, soft layer of hair, called the lanugo. This is sometimes still present at birth.

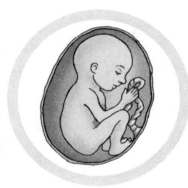

20 weeks old – half way through pregnancy.

Placenta (afterbirth)

The baby floats in shock-absorbing amniotic fluid in the womb and cannot breathe or eat. It takes oxygen and nutrients from its mother through the placenta. This is a dinner-plate-sized organ which forms in the womb wall. Inside it, oxygen and nutrients pass from the mother's blood through very thin separating sheets (membranes) into the baby's blood. The blood flows to and fro along the curly umbilical cord. After birth this is cut off or shrivels away and its stump forms the baby's navel or tummy-button.

Mother and health care

The mother's first sign of pregnancy is usually a missed period. Pregnancy tests can be done about two or three weeks after this (four to five weeks after fertilization). These check for substances (hormones) in the urine. The enlarging womb begins to show as a growing bump from three to four months. By the fifth month the mother can usually feel the baby moving, kicking and hiccuping.

In Britain mothers usually have a routine ultrasound scan when the foetus is about 18-22 weeks old. This shows an image of the baby and checks that all is well. It may also show whether the baby is a girl or boy.

Mothers are advised to attend the local health centre for regular ante-natal (before birth) check-ups. The specialist care of mothers during pregnancy and birth is known as obstetrics. The highly qualified nurses who specialize in this area are called midwives.

PUBERTY

See also Acne, Growing, Hormones, Periods and Menstrual Cycle,
Pituitary Gland, Sexual Organs, Spots and Skin Marks

Adolescence is the time during which a child grows into an adult, and undergoes many social changes, as well as changes in relationships within the family. It usually covers most of the teenage years. Within this time is puberty, when the body grows physically, changing from a child's to an adult's.

Puberty is accompanied by changes in thoughts, feelings and behaviour. In particular, puberty involves the full development of the sexual organs – the only body system that does not work during childhood. Puberty is controlled by the release of hormones, especially from the pituitary gland under the brain. Puberty usually happens to girls from about the age of 11 and to boys

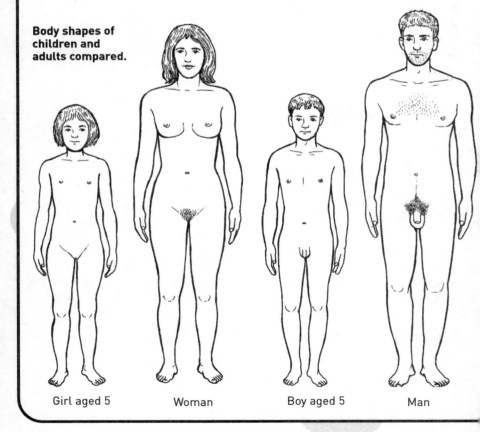

Body shapes of children and adults compared.

Girl aged 5   Woman   Boy aged 5   Man

from about the age of 13. The timing can be affected by body size and weight, genes that run in the family, a serious illness or other events. The changes usually take two to three years for girls, and three to four for boys. Some worry greatly that they are early or late developers. But this is almost always part of the natural variation between individuals.

Serious development problems are extremely rare. Most doctors advise attention if there are no signs at all of puberty by 14 years of age. Any problems that do occur can usually be treated with hormone injections.

Puberty for girls

Girls go through a sequence of changes which include the following:

• Breasts grow and develop (budding). Sometimes one breast grows before the other. This is often the first sign of puberty.

• Pubic hair grows between the legs and hair grows under the arms.

• There is rapid gain in height (the growth spurt).

• Periods begin. This is the start of menstruation and is called the menarche.

• The body's outline changes from an angular childhood shape to become more rounded, especially around the shoulders and hips.

• The voice deepens slightly.

Puberty for boys

The general sequence of changes for boys includes:

• Growth of the sexual organs, testes and penis. The penis may become stiff or erect, perhaps as part of sexual excitement but often for no obvious reason.

• Pubic hair grows between the legs as well as hair under the arms.

• There is a rapid gain in height (the growth spurt).

• The body's outline changes from an angular childhood shape, muscles become larger, shoulders wider and hips narrower.

• Ejaculation is possible, which means the release from the penis of seminal fluid containing sperm.

• The voice deepens (or breaks).

A difficult time

Young people going through puberty often feel awkward and clumsy as their bodies, especially their limbs, grow fast. Hormonal changes can cause skin spots and acne at a time when looks and appearance become more important. Often, friends seem less troubled by puberty, and in general, life often seems unfair. But in fact the changes of puberty affect everyone, most young people feel the same about them, and the worries soon fade as life begins to grow more interesting.

PULSE

See also Blood, Blood Vessels, Heart and Pulse

Every time your heart beats a surge of pressure pushes blood into the vessels called arteries. Each artery widens as a bulge or pulse of blood moves along it. This happens all over the body, but the usual place to feel the throbbing is the radial artery on the inside of the wrist, below the thumb mound. Trained people may feel for a pulse in the neck or other places. Your pulse rate records the number of heartbeats per minute.

RADIOTHERAPY

See also Cancer, Health Workers, Hospitals

Radiotherapy is treatment by radiation – usually in the form of electromagnetic waves such as invisible radio waves, microwaves, X-rays and gamma rays. Machines controlled by radiotherapists direct these beams very accurately to kill unwanted microscopic cells, tissues, growths and cancers. Sometimes the radiation comes from a wire or pellet put into the body.

RASHES

See also Allergies, Chickenpox, Dermatitis, Ezcema, Germs and Infection, Measles, Meningitis, Rubella, Skin and Touch, Spots and Skin Marks, Shingles

A rash is a change in skin colour, which might become redder or darker. The skin might also change in texture, for example becoming spotty or lumpy. A rash might be itchy, and the skin may be flaky, crusty, sore or weeping. The rash might cover one small area or spread over most of the body. Dozens of disorders have their own types of rashes, including infections such as measles and chickenpox. They can also be caused by allergies and eczema, reactions to powerful chemicals such as cleansers, or by a nettle sting. An unusual or unexplained rash should be shown to a doctor.

RECTUM

See also Intestines, Stomach and Digestion

The rectum is the last portion of the digestive tract (tube) through the body. It is about 15 cm long and stores the leftovers from digestion, known by various names, including faeces, bowel motions and poo, before these leave through the anus.

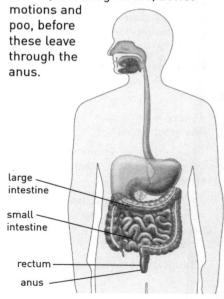

large intestine

small intestine

rectum

anus

The rectum is the last part of the bowel.

REFLEXES

See also Brain and Thinking, Eyes and Seeing, Knee, Muscles, Sneezing

A reflex is a fast automatic reaction or movement by the body, usually as a response to something happening near or on it. Reflex actions often happen before we realize or try to stop them.

Examples of reflexes

• Blinking, a reflex which washes dust from the eyes.

• The pupil reflex: the iris (the coloured part of the eye) makes the hole inside it (the pupil) larger or smaller. This stops too much bright light entering the eye in bright conditions, which might damage the delicate retina inside the eye.

•The withdrawal reflex, which pulls a body part away from anything unusual or painful, such as a thorn pricking the skin.

• The knee-jerk reflex, when the knee straightens if the tendon just below the knee cap is tapped.

Paramedics check victims' reflexes to find out how extensively they are injured and also assess their level of consciousness. This is often done by shining light from a small torch into the eyes. A doctor may test a person's reflexes to check for nerve damage or muscle disease.

RESPIRATION

See also Cells, Tissues and Organs, Lungs and Breathing, Oxygen

The word respiration has several meanings:

•The physical movements of breathing - inhaling air into the lungs, and then exhaling it.

• The process of obtaining oxygen from the air and carrying it around in the blood to all body parts.

•The chemical changes inside microscopic cells which break apart glucose, or blood sugar, to release energy for powering the cell's life processes. This is called cellular respiration.

Aerobic exercise

During aerobic exercise (meaning exercise with oxygen) the heart and lungs work faster to provide extra oxygen and blood glucose for increased cellular respiration. This is part of the health benefits of such exercise, by making the heart and lungs work harder. You can feel this as a faster pulse rate and quicker, deeper breathing.

Anaerobic exercise

Anaerobic exercise (meaning exercise without oxygen) is usually taken in quick bursts, uses different chemical changes within cells, and does not have the same effect on general health.

RHEUMATISM

See also Arthritis, Cartilage, Immunity and Immunizations, Joints, Muscles, Physiotherapy

The word rheumatism is a vague term for general aches and pains, especially in joints and/or muscles. The pain may be cause by conditions such as osteoarthritis, rheumatoid arthritis, sprained joints or strained muscles.

Rheumatoid arthritis makes the body's self-defence immune system attack its own joints, which become swollen, red, tender, stiff and painful, sometimes with bony lumps. Osteoarthritis makes the cartilage in a joint rough, pitted and worn, as a result of injury or overuse in earlier years.

Treatments for both include physiotherapy, medical drugs and sometimes surgery to remove worn parts or put in an artificial joint.

RIBS

See also Bones and Skeleton, Lungs and Breathing

The 24 long, springy rib bones arch from the backbone around the chest to the breastbone. They form a cage which protects the heart and lungs. The front part of each rib, where it joins to the breastbone, is not true bone but strong costal cartilage.

A broken rib, after a check-up, is usually left to heal itself – unless it sticks into or punctures a lung, which is an emergency.

WHAT PEOPLE SAY

Women have one fewer pair of ribs than men.

No. Both men and women have 12 pairs of ribs.

RUBELLA

See also Germs and Infections, Immunity and Immunizations, Rashes, Spots and Skin Marks

Rubella is a rarely serious viral infection, also called German measles. It causes sneezing, coughing, a sore throat, swollen glands, slight fever and a rash of pink lumps on the skin. Cases of rubella are rare as most people are vaccinated against it by the MMR vaccine. But if a woman catches it in the early stage of pregnancy, her baby may not develop properly. So any illness which may be rubella should be reported to a doctor.

SALIVA
See also Carbohydrates, Enzymes, Food and Eating, Glands, Mumps, Teeth

Also called spit, saliva is made by six salivary glands – one just below and in front of each ear, one under each side of the tongue, and one in each angle of the jaw. Each gland's tube (or duct) opens into the mouth. We produce about a litre of saliva daily, which moistens food as we chew and swallow, and contains enzymes to digest carbohydrates (mainly starches).

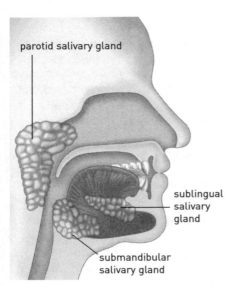

parotid salivary gland

sublingual salivary gland

submandibular salivary gland

There are three salivary glands on each side of the face.

SARS
See also Bronchitis, Influenza, Lungs and Breathing, Pneumonia

Severe Acute Respiratory Syndrome (SARS) is a rare virus infection that affects the lungs and breathing. After a world outbreak in 2003, most cases now occur in Central and East Asia. People who travel abroad and then develop high fever, a dry cough, shortness of breath, wheezing, and also perhaps headache, body aches and diarrhoea, should report urgently to a doctor.

SCANS
See also Hospitals, X-rays

Many kinds of scans send rays or beams through the body to produce computer-generated images (pictures) of the inside. Most scans show soft parts of the body, such as nerves and blood vessels, which ordinary X-rays do not. Scans are used to assess injuries and look for growths, blood clots and signs of disease.

Types of scans

•CT (CAT, Computerized Axial Tomography) uses very weak X-rays to show sections or slices of the body.

• MRI (NMR, Nuclear Magnetic Resonance Imaging) uses a combination of strong magnetism and radio waves to give a detailed view.

• Ultrasound detects the reflections or echoes of very high-pitched sound waves. This is the routine scan during pregnancy for an unborn baby.

• Echocardiography uses a similar ultrasound process to follow the movements of the beating heart.

125

SCHIZOPHRENIA
See also Brain and Thinking, Psychiatrist

Schizophrenia is sometimes called split personality, but a better description might be shattered mind. The name covers a range of mental problems which affect the way someone thinks and behaves. About one person in 100 has schizophrenia and it usually begins to affect them between the ages of 15 to 30.

Problems and treatment

Schizophrenia is a complicated and difficult condition. It seems to run in families, but its causes are not clear. It is also very variable. An affected person may withdraw from daily life and be very quiet – or may often get into arguments. Sometimes people have problems with simple activities such as eating, drinking and sleeping, and so they need constant help.

The main treatments are various types of medical drugs called antipsychotics or major tranquillizers. Some patients need 24-hour care in special centres, to make sure they take their medication regularly.

SENILITY AND DEMENTIA
(including Alzheimer's)

Senility is an older term for what we now usually call dementia. Senile dementia affects people after the age of 65 years, and pre-senile dementia begins before 65.

But the exact age of a person is usually less important than the type and cause of dementia, and the effect it has on the individual and his or her family, friends and other people.

People with dementia usually have difficulty with thought processes and find it hard to remember, solve problems, or think in an abstract way (eg to understand someone else's point of view). This can happen naturally to a degree in older age. But tests can identify when someone is suffering from dementia.

Causes include brain diseases such as Alzheimer's and Pick's disease, long-term drug misuse or abuse, and infections, strokes and brain tumours. Some of these can be treated or even cured, but diseases such as Alzheimer's are generally not treatable.

SENSES
See also Balance, Ears and Hearing, Eyes and Seeing, Nose and Smell, Skin and Touch, Tongue and Taste

The body's best-known senses are sight, hearing, smell, taste and touch. But there are other senses too. Tiny sensors deep in the ears detect the pull of gravity and also head motion, and help with balance. Microscopic stretch sensors in muscles, tendons and ligaments tell us about the positions of our body parts. The body's temperature control system uses temperature sensors in and around the brain, and tiny pressure sensors in main blood vessels monitor blood pressure.

SEX AND SEXUAL ORGANS
See pages 128-129, 130-131

SEXUAL REPRODUCTION
See also Pregnancy, Sex, Sexual Organs

Sexual reproduction is the joining of a tiny egg cell from a woman and a microscopic sperm cell from a man, at fertilization. This forms an embryo that develops in the womb as a new baby. The egg and sperm usually come together after sex (sexual intercourse) between mother and father. But there are various other methods. Fertilization can take place outside the womb in IVF (in-vitro fertilization), often called the test-tube baby technique. Sometimes a baby develops in the womb of another woman. She is a surrogate mother, and not the natural or biological mother (who is the woman who provided the egg).

SHINGLES
See also Chickenpox, Germs and Infection, Herpes, Viruses

Shingles is an infection by the virus Herpes zoster, which also causes chickenpox. It usually affects an area of skin, producing small fluid-filled spots, and the nerves beneath, causing intense pain. This often happens on the chest, following the line of a rib, or perhaps on the face or sexual organs. Shingles becomes more common with old age and its main treatment is an anti-viral drug.

SHOULDER
See also Bones and Skeleton, Dislocations, Joints, Sprains

The shoulder's ball-and-socket design makes it one of the body's most flexible joints. But this also means it can be sprained or dislocated, where the ball-shaped upper end of the arm bone (humerus) slips out of the shallow socket formed by the shoulder blade (scapula) and collar bone (clavicle). This causes great pain and should only be treated by an expert.

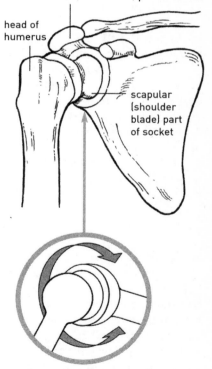

clavicular (collar bone) part of socket

head of humerus

scapular (shoulder blade) part of socket

The ball-and-socket design allows movement up and down, backwards and forwards, and twisting (rotation).

127

SEX

See also AIDS and HIV, Contraception, Fertilization, Periods and Menstrual Cycle, Pregnancy, Sexual Organs, Sexual Reproduction

The term sex has many different meanings. Women are the female sex and men are the male sex. Sex can also mean sexual intercourse, when people's sexual or genital organs touch. Full sexual intercourse happens when a man puts his erect penis into a woman's vagina. The penis may release (or ejaculate) sperm.

Homosexual or gay sex means having sex with someone who is the same sex as yourself. Women homosexuals are lesbians. Sex can involve other body parts as well as the sexual organs, for example, the mouth in oral sex.

What's not full sex?

Usually stroking, rubbing, fondling and kissing body parts are not considered as sex, unless the sexual organs are involved. If they are, but full sexual intercourse does not happen, these actions are known as known as sexual contact or sexual activity. They may happen during the time known as foreplay, when excitement and emotions rise, before full sexual intercourse.

What is sex for?

The biological reason for sex is to breed or reproduce. Sex transfers sperm cells from a man to a woman, so a sperm can join with (fertilize) an egg and start the development of a baby. The female menstrual cycle means this usually can happen only during a few days in the middle of the menstrual cycle when a ripe egg is released. This is often about day 14 (counting the day the last period started as day 1). The urge to reproduce is so basic and powerful that people may experience very intense and complicated emotions during sex. They may behave very differently from the way we might expect them to behave .

Views on sex

Many people have strong views and opinions about sex. Some religious, ethnic and cultural groups believe that people should only have sex in order to conceive babies, and otherwise it should be avoided. Others advise that sex should not begin until two partners are in an official or legal long-term relationship such as marriage.

Some people view sex as a casual event and fun, and do not want to limit themselves to one sexual partner. In contrast, others regard sex as very precious and the ultimate expression of deep love for their lifelong partner. So sex is a very individual matter. But whatever your view, sex has two possible outcomes which can change lives. These are pregnancy, and the risk of catching sexually-transmitted diseases, including HIV and AIDS.

Sex and disease

Some infections, called sexually-transmitted diseases (STDs) or venereal diseases (VDs) can be caught by having sexual intercourse or sexual contact with an infected partner. These include genital herpes, genital warts, pubic lice, syphilis, gonorrhoea, chlamydia, hepatitis B and HIV/AIDS. Some STDs can be passed on in other ways besides sex.

Some STDs cause symptoms only in the body's sexual parts, while others cause symptoms of illness throughout the body, such as skin rash and swollen glands. People who practise safe sex usually use a condom (sheath). This avoids pregnancy and reduces the areas where the sexual organs touch, which lowers the risk of spreading infection.

Sex sells

Yes it does. Many adverts use sexy people and hints about sex to grab our attention and persuade us to buy a particular product. The same can happen in daily life. This shows how widespread and basic sex is.

WHAT PEOPLE SAY

If we can't have sex, then we can't be in love.
This is not neccessarily true. Love and sex are not the same. Sex is a very personal matter for every individual and some people are more interested in it than others.

SEXUAL ORGANS

See also Babies and Infants, Birth, Bladder, Fertilization, Glands, Hormones, Ovaries Penis, Periods and Menstrual Cycle, Pregnancy, Puberty, Sex, Testes, Urine

The body's main sexual parts or organs are those involved in reproduction or making babies. They form the only body system that differs greatly between the sexes. Although there are obvious differences between women and men, there are some similarities in their reproductive parts.

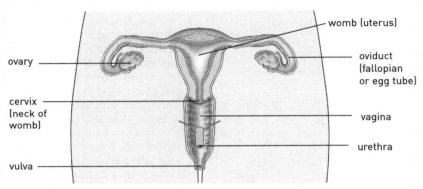

ovary

cervix (neck of womb)

vulva

womb (uterus)

oviduct (fallopian or egg tube)

vagina

urethra

The female sex organs are all within the lower abdomen (tummy).

The main sex organs for both men and women are glands (gonads) making tiny cells for reproduction, which are released into tubes. Woman's glands are the ovaries, which release egg cells into the oviducts (fallopian, egg or uterine tubes). Men have testes (testicles) which release sperm cells into the vas deferens (ductus deferens or sperm tubes). These processes are controlled by sex hormones: for women mainly by oestrogen from the ovaries and for men by testosterone from the testes.

Female sexual organs

Women have two egg-making ovaries on either side of the lower abdomen. Each is joined by its

oviduct to the pear-shaped womb or uterus. The lowest part of the womb has an opening or neck called the cervix. This leads into the tunnel-like vagina or birth canal, which opens to the outside of the body at the vulva.

DID YOU KNOW?

FEMALE
- A baby girl is born with up to half a million egg cells in her ovaries.
- By puberty the number of eggs has reduced to 200,000.
- About 500 egg cells are released during a woman's fertile years (the years when she can have babies).

130

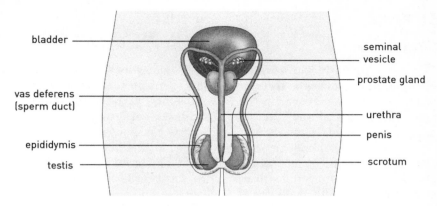

The male sex organs are mostly outside the lower abdomen (tummy).

The vulva has two pairs of lip-like folds called the labia.

During a woman's menstrual cycle a ripe egg cell from one ovary is released about every four weeks. The cell takes a day or two to pass along the oviduct. If the egg cell meets a sperm cell it may be fertilized. In the meantime the womb's inner lining has become thick and blood-rich so that it can nourish a developing baby. If the egg is not fertilized, it flows out with the womb lining through the cervix and vagina, as bleeding called a period (menstruation).

Male sexual organs

Men have two sperm-making testes which hang between their legs in a skin bag called the scrotum. Each testis is a mass of tiny tubes which makes millions of sperm every day. Next to it is a long, tightly-coiled, sperm-storing tube called the epididymis. When sperm are released they pass from the epididymis along the vas

deferens tube to the prostate just below the bladder. Here the two vas deferens join and pass the sperm into the urethra, which is the main tube from the bladder to outside the body.

The sperm are joined by a milky fluid, semen, from the prostate and two small seminal glands (vesicles) just above it. The sperm in their fluid then pass along the urethra which is inside the penis. Sperm are pumped by muscle contractions out of the end of the penis, which is called ejaculation.

DID YOU KNOW?

MALE
• If the tiny seminiferous tubules making up one testis were joined end to end they would stretch over 100 metres.
• The coiled epididymis next to each testis is about 6 metres long.
• Normally about 300-500 million sperm are released during an ejaculation.

SICKNESS

See also Food Poisoning, Stomach and Digestion, Vomiting

This is a vague term with several meanings. Someone who feels sick or has a sickness usually feels ill in a general way from almost any kind of disease. On the other hand someone feeling sick may be nauseous or queasy and about to vomit – throw up or regurgitate the contents of their stomach. This kind of being sick may be a sign of food poisoning, which can cause both sickness and diarrohea. Vomiting several times over a day or two loses valuable body fluids and minerals, especially in babies, and needs medical attention.

SIDS

See also Cot Death

Sudden Infant Death Syndrome, SIDS, or cot death, is a mysterious and tragic condition. A seemingly healthy baby dies suddenly, usually during sleep. Most affected babies are aged between two and six months old. Parents are advised to take precautions such as putting a baby to sleep on its back rather than its front, and making sure the baby is not too hot, which has helped to lower the number of cases. The condition has no clear single cause and cannot be predicted.

In very rare cases two or more babies in the same family are affected, which suggests there may be some genetic or inherited cause.

SINUSES

See also Colds and the Common Cold, Headache, Nose and Smell

The sinuses are sponge-like air spaces inside some of the bone of the face, at the front of the skull. They are connected by narrow passages to the main air spaces inside the nose. They shake or vibrate with sounds from the vocal cords and help to give every person a unique voice.

Sinus linings may become swollen, for example, when germs spread as part of a common cold. This causes soreness and the pain of a headache, usually in the frontal sinuses in the forehead, or the maxillary sinuses in the cheek area.

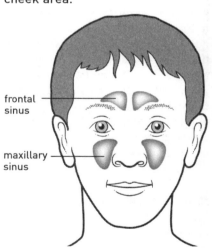

frontal sinus

maxillary sinus

The sinuses are spongy air spaces in the facial bones.

SKELETON
See pages 26–27

SKIN
See pages 134–135

SLEEP
See also Dreams and Daydreams

No one knows exactly why we sleep. But we do know what happens if people don't have enough sleep – headaches, confusion, poor memory and judgement, depression, and seeing or sensing things which aren't there (hallucinations). Being unable to sleep properly, called insomnia, stresses the body and increases the risk of catching illnesses and infections.

Sleep needs and types

Most people benefit from a long stretch of sleep at night rather than napping and dozing at odd times. People tend to need less sleep as they grow older: new babies need about 20 hours, but the average adult only seven or eight hours. However, individuals' sleep needs vary widely.

There are two main kinds of sleep. Usually the night starts with non-REM (non-Rapid Eye Movement) or deep sleep. Heartbeat, breathing, digestion and other processes slow down. Muscles relax. The body's repair of everyday wear and tear increases. This type of sleep happens between periods of REM sleep, when the body speeds up slightly, muscles twitch, and the eyes flick about under closed lids. Dreams happen mainly during REM sleep.

Guidelines for sleeping well

These guidelines may seem obvious but some people still ignore them.

• Don't take cat-naps during the day.

• Set a regular time when you go to sleep.

• During the hour before settling down to sleep avoid watching exciting programmes such as horror movies or playing computer games, or reading adventure novels. Don't have drinks which contain stimulants, such as coffee and tea, or fizzy drinks.

• Make sure your sleeping place is quiet, dark, and not too cold or hot.

• Try to switch off from problems you can't think through and act on while in bed at night. Put them to one side to solve when you are fresh in the morning.

•Think about pleasant memories or plans, such as holidays and good times.

SKIN AND TOUCH

See also Acne, Burns, Eczema, Freckles, Hair, Melanin, Moles, Nails,
Personal Hygiene, Rashes, Senses, Spots and Skin Marks, Sunburn, Sweat

Although it is thin and spread out, skin is the body's largest single organ (main part). Information on many of its features, such as colour, freckles and moles, and problems such as eczema, rashes and spots, is given on other pages.

Skin's many roles

• Skin provides our sense of touch.

• Skin physically protects delicate parts underneath from knocks and scrapes.

• Skin keeps in vital body fluids.

• Skin keeps out dust and dirt.

• Skins protects the inner body against the sun's harmful ultraviolet and other rays.

• Skin gets rid of small amounts of waste substances through sweat.

• Skin makes some vitamins when sun shines on it, mainly vitamin D which gives us strong bones and teeth.

• Skin helps to keep the body at a constant healthy temperature by several methods, as explained below.

Temperature control

When temperatures are low, the skin reduces the blood flowing through it, so less blood heat is lost from the skin's surface. This makes people look paler. The skin also has tiny body hairs which stand upright to trap more heat-retaining air near the surface.

When body temperature is high the skin's blood flow increases so more warmth is lost from the skin's surface. This makes the skin look redder or flushed. The tiny body hairs lie flat to trap less heat-retaining air near the surface. And the skin's sweat glands release watery sweat which draws heat from the body as it dries.

Skin structure

Skin has two layers, the outer epidermis and the inner dermis. The epidermis is thinner, except in areas of pressure and wear such as the soles of the feet. Microscopic cells in the base of the epidermis constantly multiply and pass outwards as they fill with the tough, hard substance keratin. The cells reach the skin's surface where they are rubbed or worn away. The whole epidermis renews itself every month.

The lower layer, the dermis, is strengthened by micro-fibres of collagen and elastin. It contains follicles from which hairs grow, as well as sweat glands, microscopic capillary blood vessels and micro-sensors for touch.

Touch

The dermis contains more than 100 million microscopic touch sensors or corpuscles of different shapes. Pacinian sensors are the largest (up to half a millimetre), look like tiny onions in the base of the dermis, and respond to heavy pressure. Meissner's sensors are much smaller and flatter. They are at the top of the dermis and respond to very light touch. Free nerve endings have branches like tiny trees and feel touch, temperature and pain. Using these and other sensors, we can detect not just physical contact, but also the amount of pressure, movements, heat and cold, dry or wet surfaces, and surface texture (rough or smooth).

Skin care

Most people usually need to wash their skin with a mild soap every day. Dry skin tends to flake and crack and can be eased by moisturizing creams. Wrinkles appear naturally with age as the elastin micro-fibres in skin become less stretchy. This is more likely to happen if skin has been exposed to much sunlight over the years. Some creams make wrinkles less obvious for a time, but cannot cure them permanently.

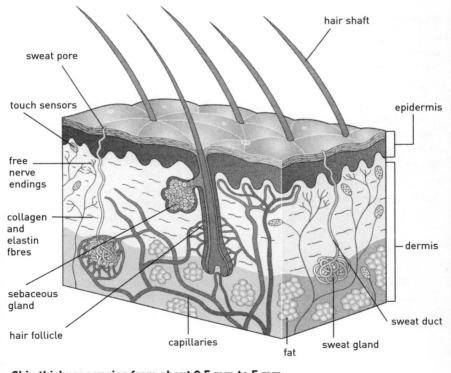

sweat pore

hair shaft

touch sensors

epidermis

free nerve endings

collagen and elastin fbres

sebaceous gland

dermis

hair follicle

capillaries

fat

sweat gland

sweat duct

Skin thickness varies from about 0.5 mm to 5 mm.

SMELL

See also Bad Breath, Body Odour, Nose and Smell, Personal Hygiene, Senses

Smell is one of the body's main senses, and detects tiny particles called odorants floating in air. It can warning us that food is bad or detect smoke from a fire. It also gives us pleasure, for example, by detecting the scent of flowers, perfumes and delicious food. We can become used to smells, which means that after we first detect them, they seem to fade – even though they are still present. This can lead to the problem of not noticing our own body odours or bad breath.

SNEEZING

See also Colds and the Common Cold, Germs and Infection, Hay Fever, Nose and Smell, Reflexes

A sneeze is an automatic action or reflex, which expels (gets rid of) substances that are irritating or blocking the inside of the nose. The lungs take in extra air, the tongue blocks off the mouth, and the breathing muscles blast air out of the nose faster than an

DID YOU KNOW?

When you sneeze, your eyelids close to stop your eyeballs rattling in their sockets, and your heart stops for a second.

express train. If you feel a sneeze coming, try to blow your nose into a paper tissue or handkerchief first. A sneeze sprays tiny drops of mucus and germs into the air for several metres, and other people may breathe them in.

SOLVENTS

See also Drugs, Health Risks, Lungs and Breathing

Solvents are chemical substances that can evaporate or change from liquid into gas or fumes. Some people breathe them in as a form of drug misuse. This can cause rashes and spots around the nose and face. Breathing solvents can also result in loss of control over the body's movements, so there is a greater risk of having an accident, or even dying.

SMOKING

See also Cancers, Drugs, Health Risks, Lungs and Breathing, Tobacco

Smoking involves taking drugs such as tobacco, cannabis or crack cocaine by breathing in or inhaling smoke and fumes from them as they burn. In addition to the dangers from the drugs themselves, any kind of smoke and hot fumes can damage the lungs, causing a long list of health problems from coughs to cancers. For example, as the hot air in the smoke passes through the windpipe and deep into the airways of the lungs, it scorches the microscopic hairs, cilia, in their lining. Cilia normally wave or beat to remove the natural mucus (phlegm) in the lining that traps bits of dust and germs. So the airways are more likely to become clogged with old germ-laden mucus. Also, tiny particles in the smoke settle into the airway linings and cause further damage.

SPINA BIFIDA

See also Bones and Skeleton, Nerves, Scans, Vitamins

A baby born with spina bifida has a spinal column or backbone which has not formed properly. The backbone does not fully enclose the body's main nerve, the spinal cord, which may poke out from it along the back.

Some babies have just a slight dimple in their backs. Others have a spinal cord covered only by thin skin. Their lower body may be paralysed and they may not be able to control their bladder or bowels. The severe form of the condition is very difficult to treat and a baby born with spina bifida may need several operations.

The causes of spina bifida are not known. About one case in 20 occurs in a family with a history of spina bifida – but the rest do not. Scientists know that a substance called folic acid (also known as folate, or vitamin B9 or M) can help to prevent it. Surveys show that women who take around 400 micrograms of folic acid daily can reduce the risk of having a baby with spina bifida by two-thirds. Women should ask for medical advice before doing this.

SPLEEN

See also Blood, Germs and Infection, Immunity and Immunizations, Lymph Fluid and Glands, Stitch

The spleen is a fist-sized organ behind the lower stomach, near the left kidney. It is part of the blood and lymph systems. It helps to filter and clean blood, store and break down old red blood cells, and store and make new white blood cells to fight germs and infections. If the spleen is injured in an accident it can bleed a lot, which may have serious results. The spleen can be removed if it is diseased or enlarged, usually with only small effects on the body's general health.

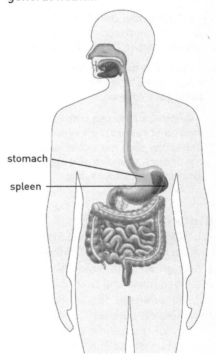

stomach

spleen

The spleen is in the rear of the upper left abdomen.

SPOTS AND SKIN MARKS

See also Acne, Allergies, Birthmarks, Bites and Stings, Bruises, Boils, Cold Sores, Eczema, Freckles, Moles, Personal Hygiene, Puberty, Rashes, Skin and Touch, Sunburn, Tattoos and also infections such as Chickenpox, Measles, Rubella, Shingles

Spots, pimples, marks and rashes on the skin occur for a variety of reasons. Some are there at birth, as birthmarks, or are natural variations in the skin's colour, such as freckles and moles.

• Spots and pimples are often the result of being a teenager when they are caused by the changing hormones of puberty, as acne.

• Rashes and spots can be the result of infection by germs, either in the skin itself or as a general illness affecting the whole body such as chickenpox.

• Allergies can causes rashes and spots, for example some forms of eczema, as well as food allergies.

• Spots can be the result of not washing the skin and poor personal hygiene.

• General stress can also cause spots and rashes, as a result of an unhealthy diet, not enough sleep, not enough exercise and activity, and worry and depression.

Blackheads

A blackhead (comedone) starts in a tiny pit or follicle from which a hair grows, and which also has a sebaceous gland that makes sebum – natural oils and waxes to keep skin supple. The opening or pore of the follicle and sebaceous gland can be blocked by a plug of hardened sebum.

More sebum collects beneath as a small swelling or bulge, and dirt is mixed into the plug as the blackhead. Less often a spot can become infected with pus, when it is called a boil.

What to do

Most skin spots and marks are quickly identified and soon fade. Scratching can make them worse as it opens the skin to germs and may cause scars. If a skin mark stays for more than a few days for no obvious reason, it's best shown to a doctor.

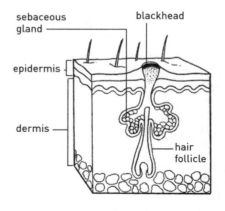

Cutaway view of a blackhead.

SPORT

See also Exercise and Fitness,
Health Risks, Muscles

Sports vary in activity level from gentle bowls and croquet to highly-energetic water polo and mountain bike racing. They need varying amounts of equipment too, ranging from a patch of level ground to an Olympic-sized swimming pool. They also vary widely in cost: jogging in the park is cheaper than flying off to ski slopes.

The choice of sports is vast: it is best to try as many different sports as possible to find one you like. Participating regularly in a sport will mean you are fitter and healthier as a result. Sport can teach us a great deal about motivation, commitment, how to be a team member, how to be a good loser, and how not to be an arrogant, big-headed winner.

SPRAINS

See also Joints, Dislocations, Hip, Knee,
Ligaments, Muscles, Shoulder

A sprained joint has been bent or wrenched too far or in the wrong direction. This stretches the muscles, ligaments and other parts inside the joint. It swells, stiffens and aches, and needs rest and support, such as strapping with a bandage. The pain should begin to ease within a day or two. If not, or if the joint is obviously out of shape, with almost no movement and sharp pains, it may be dislocated and need urgent medical attention.

STITCHES

See also Cramps, Operations, Spleen

Stitches or sutures are used to hold body parts together while they heal, such as the edges of a skin wound, or the cut ends of inner organs after an operation. Some stitches dissolve naturally (biodegrade), others need to be removed when the wound has healed. To avoid puckering and scars, various clips, adhesive strips or 'butterflies' may be used instead.

Another meaning of the word stitch is a sharp pain in the left side, usually when the body is not used to exercise. This may be caused by muscle cramps or by the spleen releasing stored blood cells into the blood system.

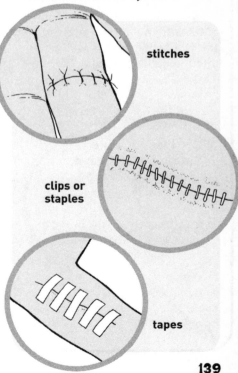

stitches

clips or staples

tapes

STOMACH AND DIGESTION

See also Diets and dieting, Energy, Enzymes, Flatulence, Food and Eating,
Food Poisoning, Glands, Gullet, Indigestion, Intestines, Saliva, Ulcers, Vomiting

Digestion is the breakdown of foods into tinier and tinier pieces, until they are small enough to take into the body and use for energy, growth and repair. The food is both physically squashed and mashed, and chemically attacked and dissolved. Both these processes start in the mouth, as chewing mixes food with saliva. The mushy food is swallowed down the gullet into the stomach, a J-shaped bag next to the liver. This can stretch as food and drink enter, to hold a volume of two litres, or more.

The stomach's walls have three layers of sheet-like muscles. These contract in waves and make it squirm and writhe, to squeeze and squash the food inside. Where the gullet joins the stomach is a ring of muscle, the oesophageal (cardiac) sphincter. This relaxes to let through each swallowed lump of food, then tightens again to stop the stomach contents welling up into the gullet. A similar muscle ring, the pyloric sphincter, controls digested food leaving the stomach and moving into the small intestine.

Inside the stomach

The stomach's lining has many small folds and wrinkles, and contains millions of microscopic glands which make digestive juices. Two of these are enzymes – lipase attacks fats in food, and pepsin breaks down proteins. Another gastric (stomach) juice is strong hydrochloric acid, which dissolves all kinds of foods and also helps to kill any germs which come in with food or drink. Other tiny glands in the stomach lining make thick, slimy mucus. This covers the lining and stops the stomach's powerful juices from digesting itself.

Further digestion

Food usually stays in the stomach for between one and four hours, depending on the size and type of meal – fatty foods remain

WHAT PEOPLE SAY

I've got a big stomach so I have to eat lots of food.
Stomachs do vary in size. But eating a lot is usually linked more with appetite, habit or even greediness, rather than stomach size.

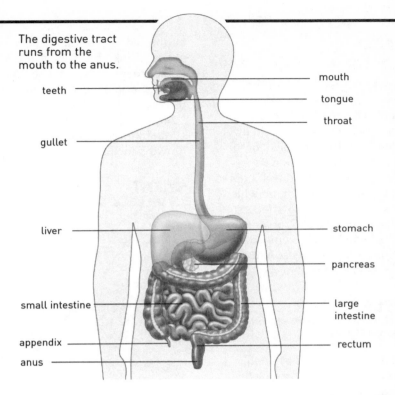

The digestive tract runs from the mouth to the anus.

teeth
gullet
liver
small intestine
appendix
anus

mouth
tongue
throat
stomach
pancreas
large intestine
rectum

for longer. By now the food is a thick soup called chyme. It oozes in small blobs into the small intestine, where more enzymes attack it. The small intestine is the main place for absorption – taking the food through the intestinal lining, into the blood stream, to be spread around the body.

The stomach absorbs little – mainly sugars and substances such as alcohol.

Aches and pains

Most digestive and stomach problems, such as food poisoning, indigestion and ulcers, are covered elsewhere. The stomach's main defence

is vomiting to rid itself of bad, rotten, poisonous or germ-contaminated food.

WHAT PEOPLE SAY

I've got terrible stomach ache! (clutching the navel or belly-button)

The stomach is not here – it's higher up, mostly behind the lower left ribs. Pain around waist level or lower is usually linked to the intestines, appendix or bladder, or for women, the womb.

STROKE
See also Brain and Thinking, Blood Vessels

During a stroke, parts of the brain do not receive a blood supply. This may be because an artery becomes blocked by a blood clot (thrombosis), or because it has a weak patch (aneurysm) in its wall that bulges and bursts. Depending on which parts of the brain are affected, the signs of a stroke range from slurred speech and confusion to collapse and paralysis. A stroke is a medical emergency.

STYE
See also Boils, Hair, Skin and Touch, Spots and Skin Marks

A stye is an infected eyelash follicle – the tiny pit from which the lash grows. The area swells and reddens, and pus collects. Bathing with warm salty water every few hours may help bring the stye to a head and release the pus, when the eyelash usually falls out too. The pus should be cleaned away carefully to avoid smearing or infecting the eye.

SUNBURN
See also Burns, Melanin, Skin and Touch

When skin is exposed to strong sunlight gradually over many days it naturally darkens until it has a protective suntan. High-factor sunscreen will help to prevent the sun's invisible ultraviolet rays making the skin red, hot, painful or even blistered. Sunburn should be treated by resting in cool shade, drinking plenty of water, and perhaps applying a soothing lotion. Serious sunburn needs urgent medical attention.

Any regular exposure to strong sunlight increases the risk of skin growths including cancers.

SWEAT
See also Glands, Skin and Touch, Temperature

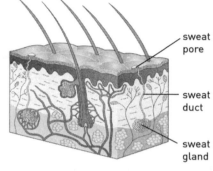

sweat pore

sweat duct

sweat gland

Sweat glands are in skin's dermis layer.

Sweat (perspiration) is a salty, watery fluid made by millions of tiny glands in the skin. As sweat dries it draws heat from the body and helps to control temperature. We sweat more when the weather is hot, especially on the forehead, hands, under the arms and between the legs – as much

DID YOU KNOW?

If the microtubes in all the body's tiny sweat glands were joined end to end they would stretch more than 10 kilometres.

as a litre of sweat can be produced in one hour. Even in cool weather the skin releases 50-70 millilitres of sweat daily. Noticeable sweating in cooler conditions can be a sign of various illnesses, which range from fever (due to infection) to a heart attack.

TASTE
See page 149

TATTOOS
See also AIDS and HIV, Hepatitis, Skin and Touch, Spots and Skin Marks

A tattoo is made by poking tiny particles of pigments (colouring substances) into one of the skin's deeper layers. The site, size, design and whether they look good are all matters of personal taste. The main health risk is infection of the site of the tattoo. This can be very serious, and include hepatitis or HIV/AIDS, so only fully registered and qualified tattooists should be used. The medical uses of tattooing include matching grafted or discoloured skin as part of cosmetic surgery.

WHAT PEOPLE SAY

My tattoo seemed like a good idea at the time. Now I wish I'd never had it.

Lots of people say this. People who are desperate for a tattoo can try a temporary one to see how they like it.

TB
See page 150

TEETH
See pages 144–145

TEMPERATURE
See also Exposure, Fever, Hypothermia, Thermometer

A healthy human body maintains a temperature of 37°C (degrees Celsius) or 98.4°F (degrees Fahrenheit), varying by perhaps one degree depending on conditions. Body temperature is taken using a medical or clinical thermometer.

High temperature or fever above about 40°C (often due to infection), usually causes sweating and can lead to dangerous heatstroke or hyperthermia. Low temperature, below about 35°C, usually causes shivering and can lead to dangerous hypothermia or exposure. Both these conditions need urgent medical attention.

TENDONS
See also Bones and Skeleton, Muscles

Tendons are strong, stringy, rope-like parts at the ends of muscles, which anchor them firmly to bones (or other tendons). If they are put under great stress they may partly tear or rupture, or even snap. This is rare but very painful and the part cannot move properly. Treatment is usually an operation to re-attach the muscle, tendon and bone.

143

TEETH

See also Abscess, Bad Breath, Dentists, Gums, Personal Hygiene

Teeth are the hardest parts of the body, which can survive a lifetime of biting and chewing. We have four kinds of teeth. At the front are incisors, straight-edged like chisels for biting and slicing. Next are canines or eye teeth, taller and more pointed, for tearing and ripping. Behind them, the premolars are wider with lumpy-looking surfaces. At the back of the mouth are the broad molars or cheek teeth. Premolars and molars crush and squash food while chewing.

A tooth has two main parts, the crown which is the visible part above the gum, and the root fixed into the jawbone. The junction between the crown and the root below is the neck, where the gum meets the tooth.

The crown's outer layer is very hard, whitish enamel. Under this is slightly softer dentine, which helps to cushion jolts and jars as we chew. In the middle of the tooth is soft dental pulp – mainly blood vessels to nourish the tooth and nerve endings which warn of pressure, heat, cold, damage and decay.

The tooth's root is fixed into the jaw with cementum or 'living glue'. The nerves and blood vessels pass out of the tooth at its lowest point, the root canal.

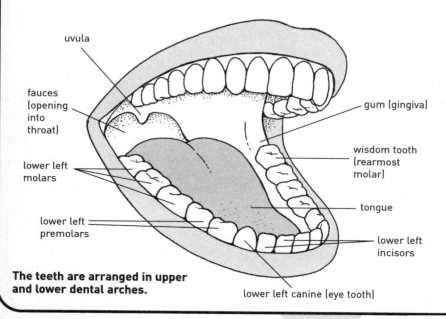

The teeth are arranged in upper and lower dental arches.

Baby teeth

We have two sets of teeth. First is the milk, baby or deciduous (falling out) set, numbering 20. In each half of each jaw there are two incisors, one canine and two molars. The first incisors usually erupt (grow above the gum) between 6 and 12 months of age, and the last molars at 2-3 years.

Adult teeth

Between about 6 and 12 years baby teeth fall out, usually in order from front to back, and adult or permanent teeth grow in their place. In this set, each half of each jaw has two incisors, one canine, two premolars and three molars, making a total of 32.

However all these ages and arrangements of teeth vary. Some people grow their four rearmost molars or wisdom teeth around the ages of 18-20. Others never grow these teeth above the gum, although they may be present as buds inside the jaw bone.

Cleaning teeth

Oral hygiene includes the health of teeth, gums (gingivae), tongue and the whole mouth. A dentist or oral hygienist can show you how to use a toothbrush and fluoride toothpaste to clean between teeth and where the teeth meet the gums, as well as making sure that all the bits of old food are removed.

Brushing is usually done in small circles and is best after meals and last thing at night.

Floss is a thin cord which can be put between the teeth to remove stuck pieces of food. Regular mouthwashes also help and freshen breath. Bacterial germs 'eat' old bits of food and make acid, which causes teeth to rot or decay. This causes bad breath (halitosis).

Check-ups and toothache

Most people are advised to see a dentist twice yearly for a check-up and treatment. Putting this off may allow any decay to worsen, and mean a greater risk of needing serious treatment. Any chips, cracks or toothache – from the tooth itself or an abscess (infection) on the gum or around the root – should be reported quickly to a dentist.

WHAT PEOPLE SAY

I didn't see the dentist because I didn't have toothache, but when I finally went I needed loads of treatment. Early treatment of tooth decay and other dental conditions keeps teeth healthy. Otherwise problems are likely to worsen. So regular check ups are important even if it seems there are no symptoms.

TESTES (TESTICLES)
See also Fertilization, Sexual Organs

The male body has two testes, held in a skin bag called the scrotum between the legs. These make sperm cells which can join egg cells to start a new baby.

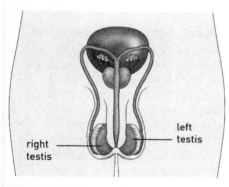

right testis

left testis

The testes are the male sex glands.

TETANUS
See also Bacteria, Germs and Infection, Immunity and Immunizations

Tetanus is a serious illness also called lockjaw, caused by Clostridium bacterial germs. These are found in soil, dirt and dust, especially where there are animal droppings and manure. They usually enter the body through a cut. Several days or weeks later the muscles stiffen and ache, including the jaw muscles, which gives the illness the name lockjaw. The breathing muscles may also stiffen which can lead to suffocation.

In the UK tetanus is rare because most children are immunized against it with the DTP vaccine (Diphtheria, Tetanus, Pertussis). People at risk, such as gardeners, park workers and farmers, may receive regular booster injections every five or ten years.

THERMOMETER
See also Fever, Hypothermia, Temperature

Body temperature is measured by a clinical or medical thermometer. This can be a rod of glass with a very narrow tube inside, containing a red or silvery liquid in a bulb. This end is placed under the tongue for a minute, then the temperature read from the end of the liquid in the tube.

Another less accurate design is a plastic strip placed on the skin, usually the forehead. Coloured patches or numbers glow to show the temperature.

A third type, based on a device called a thermocouple, is a thin rod or probe placed into a body opening such as an ear or the mouth. Wires link it to a dial or display showing the temperature. Normal body temperature is 37°C (degrees Celsius).

Why take temperature?
Body temperature is a valuable sign for indicating disease, especially infection. So hospital nurses use thermometers regularly as part of monitoring a patient's condition. One type of thermometer, which is clipped to a finger, also has a pulse recording device.

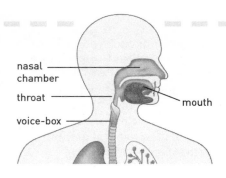

The throat is just above the voice-box (larynx) and start of the gullet.

THROAT
See also Choking, Gullet, Lungs and Breathing, Lymph Fluid and Glands, Tonsils, Voicebox and Speech

The throat (also called the pharynx) links the back of the nose and mouth above it with the windpipe (trachea) and gullet (oesophagus) below it. So the throat is a passage for air when breathing, and for food and drink when swallowing.

Usually the muscle movements of swallowing fold a flap, the epiglottis, over the top of the windpipe so that food and drink goes into the gullet rather than the windpipe. However if we try to talk and swallow at the same time, or don't concentrate, food might enter the windpipe, causing coughing and choking.

Sore throats
The usual cause of a sore throat is infection by germs, such as Streptococcus bacteria in strep throat. In the throat are lumpy-looking tonsils which are part of the body's disease-fighting immune system, and these may

redden and swell, making swallowing painful. Remedies such as sucking lozenges and gargling help to ease the soreness while the body fights the germs. But if a throat is still painful after several days, or there are other symptoms such as high fever, a doctor's attention is needed.

THYMUS GLAND
See also Blood, Glands, Immunity and Immunizations, Lymph Fluid and Glands

The thymus is a soft pink organ behind the breastbone, just in front of and above the heart. It is part of the body's self-defence immune system and helps to 'train' the white blood cells called lymphocytes so that they become ready to fight germs and disease. A baby or child has a relatively large thymus; it begins to shrink away after the teenage years.

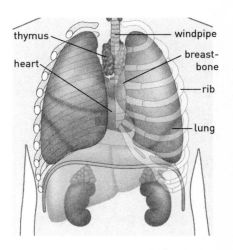

The thymus gland is protected behind the breastbone (sternum). It has two lobes, left and right, joined by connective tissue.

147

THYROID GLAND
See also Glands, Growth, Hormones, Metabolism

The thyroid is a bow-tie-shaped part under the skin of the neck, wrapped around the upper windpipe. It makes two hormones (controlling substances), thyroxine (T4) and tri-iodothyronine (T3). These affect the speed at which the body's millions of microscopic cells work (called metabolism) and how fast they use energy.

   The thyroid needs the mineral iodine to make its hormones. If the thyroid does not get enough iodine from food and drink, it grows bigger in an attempt to make more hormones. This may form a lump in the neck called a goitre.

thyroid — windpipe — voice-box

The thyroid has two parts or lobes, left and right, joined by a narrower strap.

In many regions tiny amounts of iodine are added to cooking salt so that people receive enough. Embedded in the thyroid are four tiny parathyroid glands which make a hormone that controls the mineral calcium in the blood.

TIREDNESS
See also Anaemia, Depression, ME, Muscles, Sleep

There are 101-plus causes of tiredness, from running a marathon to lack of sleep. Some people naturally have a less active, energetic approach to life. When compared to someone who is always 'on the go', they may seem tired – some might say lazy. But this can be part of the natural variation in levels of activity between individuals.

   Less commonly, tiredness is a sign of a medical condition such as anaemia or depression. Fatigue usually means physical tiredness as a result of extreme exercise or activity.

TISSUES
See also Cells, Tissues and Organs

Tissues are groups of similar microscopic cells. Examples are nervous tissue in the brain and nerves, connective tissue between and joining body parts, and epithelial tissue which forms the various coverings and linings of these parts. Another tissue is blood, which contains groups of similar cells such as red and white cells.

TOBACCO

See also Cancers, Drugs,
Health Risks, Smoking

The dried leaves of the tobacco plant are set on fire and smoked, chewed, or powdered and sniffed into the nose as snuff. Some people enjoy the activity of smoking and the buzz from the substance nicotine in the smoke. But nicotine is an addictive drug, and tobacco smoke contains dozens of harmful substances and several deadly ones. A full list of all the cancers and other diseases caused by smoking tobacco would fill many pages.

Buying tobacco in its various forms is very expensive and the smell of stale smoke lingers on hair and clothes and is very unpleasant to most people.

TONGUE AND TASTE

See also Nose and Smell, Food and Eating

The tongue's upper surface is covered with dozens of tiny 'pimples' or papillae, which help to grip food. On and between the papillae, up to 10,000 microscopic taste buds sense four basic flavours – sweet at the tongue's tip, salty along the front sides, sour along the sides at the rear, and bitter across the back. The main upper surface of the tongue has no taste buds.

The four flavours combine to give the tastes of food and drink. If a bite or ulcer on the tongue does not heal in two or three days, it should have medical attention.

TONSILS

See also Germs and Infection,
Glands, Lymph Fluid and Glands,
Nose and Smell, Throat

Tonsils are lumpy-looking, germ-fighting parts similar to lymph nodes or glands.

Everybody has three pairs of tonsils:

• Pharyngeal tonsils or adenoids, at the lower rear of the nasal chamber inside the nose

• Lingual tonsils, at the lower base of the tongue

• Palatine tonsils – which we call the tonsils – on either side of the upper throat

Tonsils swell during infection and become red, painful and enlarged as one form of sore throat – tonsillitis. Usually they shrink back to normal. But if tonsillitis keeps returning, they can be removed by an operation.

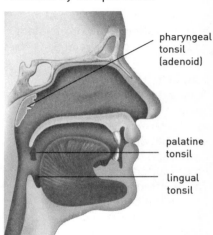

pharyngeal tonsil (adenoid)

palatine tonsil

lingual tonsil

TOUCH
See pages 134–135

TRANSPLANTS
*See also Blood, Donors, Immunity
and Immunizations, Operations*

A transplant is a body part taken from one person (the donor) and put into another (the recipient). Common transplants include blood in a blood transfusion and the cornea of the eye. Other body parts which can be transplanted include the kidneys, heart, lungs, the heart and lungs together, the liver and bone marrow.

Rejection
The recipient's immune defence system may try to attack or reject the transplant. Medical drugs called immunosuppressives can damp down this rejection, although they have side effects such as making the body less able to fight infecting germs.

Skin or bone moved from one place to another on the same person, for example, as a skin graft, is called an autotransplant and does not cause rejection.

Donating body parts
People who want to donate body parts for transplant after their death are encouraged to carry an official donor card. Their family and relatives will also be consulted after the death. This is often an emotional time, but if body parts are to be donated, they must be taken quickly.

TRAVEL SICKNESS
*See also Balance, Ear and Hearing,
Senses, Sickness, Vomiting*

Feelings of nausea or sickness, and being sick or vomiting, can be the result of the movement of boats, cars, planes and trains. This is because the brain has problems decoding nerve signals from the senses, especially the balance parts in the ears. Remedies include travel-sickness pills, not eating before a journey, and avoiding looking at nearby surroundings, but focusing on a distant steady place such as the sea's horizon or faraway fields.

TUBERCULOSIS
*See also Bacteria, BCG, Fever,
Germs and Infection, Lungs and Breathing,
Lymph Fluid and Glands*

Also called TB or consumption, tuberculosis is a serious bacterial infection that affects the lungs. It can also spread to lymph nodes (glands), intestines, kidneys, skin and other parts of the body. Early signs are fever, weight loss, night sweats and coughing up bloodstained sputum (phlegm).

TB is rare in the UK because children are protected against it by the BCG immunization, although some people may carry TB germs from other countries where it is more common. It can be treated by powerful drugs, but recovery may take some time. perhaps months. Anyone suspecting TB should see a doctor without delay.

ULCERS
See also Skin and Touch, Stomach and Digestion, Veins

An ulcer is a raw area or open sore. Skin ulcers can be the result of constant pressure, for example as bedsores. On the lower legs they are varicose ulcers. People also get ulcers in the mouth, the stomach (gastric or peptic ulcer) and the small intestine (duodenal or peptic ulcer). The treatment for skin ulcers is to keep the area clean, dry and free from pressure. Peptic ulcers are treated with various pills, including antibiotics.

URINE
See also Bladder, Cystitis, Kidneys

Urine is the waste liquid passed out from the bladder along the urethra during urination (weeing or peeing). The amount depends on how much we drink and sweat, but is usually one and a half litres per day. Urine colour varies from clear to deep yellow. Red-tinged urine may have blood in it (haematuria), and cloudy urine can be caused by germs. Both should be reported to a doctor.

VACCINATIONS
See page 88

VAGINA
See also Birth, Sex, Sexual Organs

The vagina is one of the female sexual or reproductive parts. It is like a flattened tube from the womb (uterus) to the outer body.

At birth a baby leaves its mother's womb along the vagina, so it is also called the birth canal.

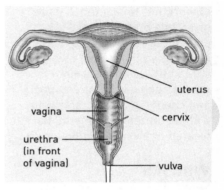

The vagina angles upwards and backwards and connects the womb to the vulval opening.

VEINS
See also Blood Vessels

Veins are wide, thin-walled, floppy tubes that carry slow-flowing, low-pressure blood to the heart. Flap-like valves inside some main veins make sure blood flows the correct way. Varicose veins have become stretched, widened and twisted. They usually occur in the lower legs, or in the anus as haemorrhoids (piles). They can be treated with creams, injections and sometimes surgery.

DID YOU KNOW?

At any single moment about three-quarters of your blood is in your veins.

151

VERRUCAS

See also Warts

Medically, a verruca is any sort of wart, but this name is usually given to a plantar wart – on the sole of the foot. Like other warts, it is caused by a virus, usually spread by walking barefoot in places such as swimming pools and changing rooms. Someone with a plantar wart should have it treated to avoid infecting others.

VIRUSES

See also Germs and Infection, Immunity and Immunization, and various viral infections such as AIDS and HIV, Chickenpox, Cold Sores, Colds and the Common Cold, Herpes, Influenza, Measles, Mumps, Rubella, Warts

Viruses are the smallest germs – one million would fit into this o. They enter the body in breathed-in air, through cuts in the skin, or in food and drink. A virus passes into one of the body's microscopic cells and makes the cell produce many copies of the virus, which are released when the cell bursts and dies. There are a few anti-viral drugs, but antibiotics do not usually work against viruses. The main weapons against them are the body's natural immune defence system and immunization with vaccines.

Many viral diseases are included in this book (see list above). Other viral illnesses include polio (poliomyelitis), cervical cancer (caused by the human papilloma virus), dengue fever, Ebola hemorrhagic fever, Lassa fever, rabies and yellow fever.

Vitamin A
Chemical name Retinol
Needed for General health, eyesight, growth, immune system

Vitamin B1
Chemical name Thiamine
Needed for Nerves, heart, muscles, digestion

Vitamin B2
Chemical name Riboflavin
Needed for Digestion

Vitamin B3
Chemical name Niacin
Needed for Brain, skin, tongue, digestion

Vitamin B6
Chemical name Pyridoxine
Needed for Digestion, growth

Vitamin B12
Chemical name Cobalamin
Needed for Digestion, growth, blood, bone marrow, nerves

VITAMINS

See also Diets and Dieting, Food and Eating

Vitamins are substances the body needs in small amounts from food to stay healthy (see table above). Many years ago various diseases were caused by a lack of vitamins, such as scurvy caused by lack of vitamin C. Today anyone who eats a varied diet, with plenty of fresh vegetables and fruit, should receive enough vitamins.

Vitamin B complex
Chemical name Folic acid
Needed for Blood, digestion

Vitamin B complex
Chemical name Biotin
Needed for Workings
of body cells

Vitamin C
Chemical name Ascorbic Acid
Needed for Teeth, bones,
blood vessels, wound healing,
protection against germs

Vitamin D
Chemical name Calciferol
Needed for Blood, teeth, bones

Vitamin E
Chemical name Tocopherol
Needed for General health,
blood

Vitamin K
Chemical name Phytomenadion
Needed for Blood clotting,
wound healing

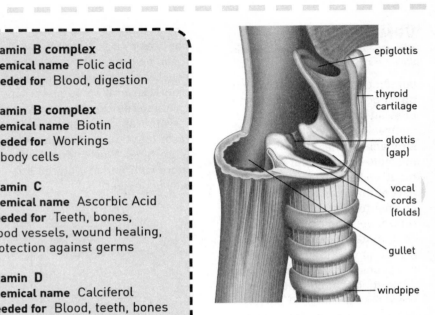

epiglottis

thyroid
cartilage

glottis
(gap)

vocal
cords
(folds)

gullet

windpipe

**The main laryngeal cartilage is
called the Adam's apple. Men have
a more angular Adam's apple than
women and children.**

VOICEBOX AND SPEECH

*See also Lungs and Breathing, Throat,
Windpipe*

The voicebox or larynx is in the
front of the neck, between the
base of the throat and the top of
the windpipe. It is made of
cartilage (gristle) plates with two
stiff flaps, one on each side, called
vocal cords or folds. Usually these
are apart leaving a V-shaped
gap, the glottis, for silently
breathing air.

Speech

When we vocalize – speak or
make other vocal-cord sounds,
such as hums and cries –
laryngeal muscles pull the vocal
cords almost together. Air passes
through the narrow gap between
them and makes them shake or
vibrate to produce sounds. Other
muscles stretch the cords to
produce sounds of higher pitch.
The mouth, nasal chamber and
sinuses alter the sounds, and
their shapes give each of us a
unique voice.

Hoarseness can be caused by
shouting too much or breathing
fumes. If it persists for several
days it may be due to small
growths such as nodules, which
should be examined by a doctor.

153

VOMITING

See also Food Poisoning, Gullet, Sickness, Stomach and Digestion

Vomiting – being sick, throwing up, chucking up – is the reverse of swallowing. Wave-like muscle contractions force food from the stomach up the gullet (oesophagus) and out of the mouth. This usually happens as part of the stomach's defence against too much food or bad, rotten, poisonous or germ-contaminated foods. It is also a common symptom of various infections and diseases.

Vomiting that continues for more than a couple of days, or even a day in babies, needs medical attention since the body loses valuable fluids, salts and minerals.

DID YOU KNOW?

Making the movements of vomiting, but not bringing up anything, is called retching.

WARTS

See also Viruses, Verrucas

Warts are small lumpy growths on the skin caused by germs called papilloma viruses. They may be like tiny mountains, or volcanoes, or lower and flat-topped. They often seem to appear for no reason – then disappear in the same way.

Any skin growth should be checked by a doctor. If it is a wart it can be removed by over-the-counter ointment or lotion (wart paint). Several small operations can also remove warts by freezing (cryotherapy), burning with a laser (cautery) or scraping out (curettage). Warts seem to be more common in children but why is unclear.

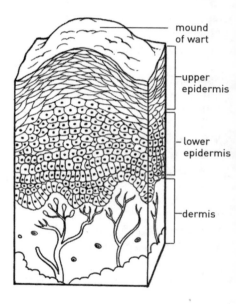

mound of wart

upper epidermis

lower epidermis

dermis

A wart is an 'overgrowth' of skin cells that occurs as a result of a viral infection.

WEIGHT

See also Anorexia and Bulimia, Calories, Diets and Dieting, Exercise and Fitness, Food and Eating, Growing, Obesity

The human body is designed to be a healthy weight for its height, throughout its growth from baby to adult, and through adulthood

154

to old age. There are small variations in body build that affect weight. But if the body is too heavy, because of too much body fat, this is called being overweight or obese. This is nearly always caused by eating too much, exercising too little, or both. Other pages describe how to check weight against height, some of the health risks of obesity, and how to diet and reduce weight.

WHAT PEOPLE SAY

I'm not overweight, just big-boned.

People vary in their bodily proportions, but the comparison called Body Mass Index (see Obesity) takes this into account. Very rarely some diseases may cause weight increase. More often people use excuses to cover up overeating.

WHEEZING
See also Asthma, Bronchitis, Lungs and Breathing, Pneumonia

Wheezy breathing is difficult and noisy, and may include panting or gasping. The sound is usually made by air passing through narrowed airways, generally the lower airways called bronchi and the smaller bronchioles deep in the lungs. Wheezing may be a sign of the allergy known as asthma, or various lung infections such as bronchitis or pneumonia, or inhaling certain fumes or smoke. A doctor can usually tell the underlying problem by checking whether the wheezing is worse on breathing in or out, listening to the chest through a stethoscope, and whether there are other symptoms such as fever and coughing.

WHOOPING COUGH
See also Bacteria, Germs and Infection, Immunity and Immunizations, Pneumonia

Whooping cough, also called pertussis, is a serious infection by the bacterial germ Bordetella pertussis. It used to affect mainly children and cause a fever, sore throat and sneezing, followed by very severe bouts of coughing. Often the cough was so relentless that the sufferer could only breathe in at the end of each bout, with a loud whooping noise, which could be followed by vomiting. This stage might last up to a month.

Risks and complications
In Britain whooping cough is now rare because most children are immunized with the DTP (Diphtheria, Tetanus, Pertussis) triple vaccine. Those children who do not receive immunization run the risk of suffering whooping cough for several weeks, and of possible complications including lung collapse and pneumonia.

155

WIND
See page 66

WINDPIPE
See also Gullet, Lungs and Breathing, Voicebox and Speech

The windpipe is also called the trachea. It is a bendy tube running from the voicebox in the front of the neck, down to the lungs in the chest. It has thousands of micro-hairs called cilia in its lining, which are coated with a thin layer of slimy, sticky mucus. The mucus traps dust and germs from breathed-in air.

The cilia hairs constantly bend or wave to make the mucus flow slowly upwards to the top of the trachea. When someone coughs slightly to clear their throat they cough up this mucus into the lower throat and swallow it into the gullet. A bigger cough brings it up into the throat as sputum or phlegm.

Any item wrapped around the neck could pull tight and squash the windpipe, leading to suffocation. Small children in particular should never play games with rope, string or scarves around the neck.

WOMB
See also Birth, Fertilization, Periods and Menstrual Cycle, Pregnancy, Sexual Organs, Vagina

The womb, or uterus, is where a baby grows and develops before birth. Usually the womb is quite small – the size and shape of a pear. Every month, as part of the menstrual cycle, its lining (endometrium) becomes thicker and blood-rich, ready to nourish a developing baby. If no baby is conceived, the lining passes out through the main opening or neck of the womb, the cervix, as a period. When a baby is conceived, the womb enlarges as it grows to accommodate the baby. At birth the baby leaves the womb through the cervix and travels along the birth canal, or vagina, to the outside world.

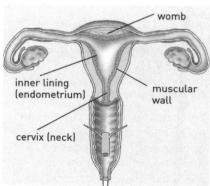

womb

inner lining (endometrium)

muscular wall

cervix (neck)

The womb is in the middle of the lower abdomen, angled or tilted forwards.

WORMS

See also Food and Eating, Intestines,
Personal Hygiene, Stomach and Digestion

Several kinds of worms can enter the body, usually as tiny and barely noticed eggs, and then grow inside. Any suspicion of worms should be reported to a doctor, since nearly all kinds can be killed with medical drugs.

Types of worms

• Tapeworms (Taenia) are long, pale flattened ribbons in the intestine.

• Roundworms in the intestine such as the pork roundworm (Ascaris) can grow as big as a pencil.

• Threadworms (pinworms, enterobiasis) are small, like wriggly lengths of cotton thread. They cause itching around the anus, especially in children at night.

• Toxocara worms from the droppings of cats and dogs are tiny, but may enter the eye and cause blindness.

Preventing worms

• Be careful about personal hygiene.

• Wash your hands after contact with dirt, soil, pet equipment and especially pet droppings.

• Ensure that all meat, especially pork, is thoroughly cooked.

WRIST

See also Bones and Skeleton,
Joints, Sprains

The wrist joint has eight small bones that slide and twist against each other. A sprained wrist hurts and swells rapidly. If there is hardly any movement in the wrist, the bones are misshapen, and there is great pain, an urgent medical check is advised since it may be broken.

X-RAYS

See also Cancers, Hospitals, Radiotherapy,
Scans

X-rays are invisible electro-magnetic energy. They pass through soft parts of the body, such as the blood and muscles, but not through bones. They are used to make pictures or radiographs of mainly bones and cartilage, for example, a broken (fractured) bone. More powerful X-rays are beamed into small areas of the body during radiotherapy, to destroy growths or tumours. Because of their powerful nature, X-rays are used by medical workers with great care. Thick layers, or shields, stop them straying and meters monitor their levels.

ZITS

See also Acne, Boils, Rashes,
Spots and Skin Marks

Zits is a common name for various kinds of spots, especially boils, pimples and blackheads.

Further reading

The Human Body: A Basic Guide to the Way You Fit Together by Moff Betts (Wooden Books/Walker & Company, 2004)

e.explore: Human Body by Richard Walker (Dorling Kindersley/Google, 2005)

The Human Body: Systems and Function by Doug Sylvester (Rainbow Horizons, 2000)

Body Focus: Injury, Illness and Health (series) by Carol Ballard and Steve Parker (Heinemann Library, 2004)

Websites

http://www.kidshealth.org/teen/
Created by doctors, with honest, accurate information and advice.

http://www.teenhealthfx.com/
Ask questions on teen health and receive personalized answers.

teens.http://www.advicehq.co.uk/Teens.htm
Loads of links for help and advice for teenagers.

http://youngminds.org.uk/young people/index.php
Articles and links for help and advice, plus further information.

INDEX

a **bold** page number indicates the main entry on a subject